FACES
of EVIL

Also by Dominic Utton

SAS Battle Ready

FACES of EVIL

Unmasking the World's Most Horrific Serial Killers

DOMINIC UTTON

Michael O'Mara Books Limited

First published in Great Britain in 2024 by
Michael O'Mara Books Limited
9 Lion Yard
Tremadoc Road
London SW4 7NQ

A CIP catalogue record for this book is available from the British Library.

Papers used by Michael O'Mara Books Limited are natural, recyclable
products made from wood grown in sustainable forests. The manufacturing
processes conform to the environmental regulations of the country of origin.

ISBN: 978-1-78929-625-9 in paperback print format
ISBN: 978-1-78929-626-6 in ebook format

1 2 3 4 5 6 7 8 9 10

Cover design by Ana Bjezancevic
Cover illustration by Cinthya Alvarez
Designed and typeset by Claire Cater
Printed and bound by CPI Group (UK) Ltd, Croydon, CR0 4YY

www.mombooks.com

MIX
Paper | Supporting
responsible forestry
FSC
www.fsc.org   FSC® C171272

CONTENTS

INTRODUCTION

They are the worst of humanity, men and women driven by an urge to kill, and kill, and kill again. They are monsters lurking among us, often living outwardly respectable lives while indulging their horrific desires under cover of darkness, or anonymity.

Some operate over years or even decades, appearing from the shadows like bogeymen before disappearing again; others indulge their murderous rages over a matter of just a few frantic, blood-soaked weeks. Some meticulously plan their attacks, selecting and stalking their victims carefully; others are opportunists, striking as and when the urge takes them.

Some carefully store the bodies of their victims in home-made graves – others simply dump them after killing, tossing the corpses aside like trash. Some take their time, prolonging the agony for as long as possible; others slaughter in a wild, furious explosion of violence.

Some kill out of rage, or revenge; others from a twisted sexual pleasure in inflicting pain. Some see killing as a kind of sport; others as a search for an ultimate existential expression. Some murder to feel powerful; others are driven by motives that remain a terrifying mystery.

All of them are the stuff of nightmares.

The official FBI classification of a serial killer is someone who murders at least three times, who targets victims previously unknown to them and who did not know each other, and who has allowed some time to elapse between each murder.

It is a definition that can be exceptionally broad. From Joanne Dennehy, the British woman who stabbed three men to death – and tried to kill another two – in 15 nightmarish days in 2013, to Samuel Little, America's deadliest serial killer, who strangled 93 women over 35 years before his eventual arrest in 2005. From Ivan Milat, who abducted, tortured and slaughtered teenage backpackers in rural Australia, to Dr Harold Shipman, the unassuming family GP who calmly administered fatal doses of painkillers to at least 218 of his elderly patients in Yorkshire and Manchester. From Dennis Nilsen, who cut up his victims and flushed their remains down the toilet, to Ted Bundy, who kept the skulls of those he killed as trophies in his apartment. From Paul John Knowles, the so-called 'Casanova Killer' who murdered between 18 and 35 times in a four-month rampage across seven American states, to Robert Hansen, who set his targets loose in the Alaskan wilderness and hunted them down like animals. All are serial killers, and all are different.

For several of these killings it took decades before policing techniques and forensic technology became advanced enough to piece together exactly what happened to the victims. Other killers were only too happy to confess their methods once caught, either from a misguided search for absolution, or out of a twisted pride in their depravity. Others still remain a tragic mystery to this day.

In this book we're going to examine the murderous careers of 20 of the most terrifying serial killers of the late twentieth and early twenty-first centuries, and – as well as unpicking their means, motives and methods – try to attempt to understand the twisted passions that drove their lust for death.

Some of these stories you may be familiar with; others you will not. Some have become household names, the subject of hit Netflix documentaries and BBC dramas; others are less well known, but no less horrifying for that.

These are the faces of evil. Don't have nightmares.

PART ONE

SHALLOW GRAVES

1

ANTHONY SOWELL

(USA, 2007–09, 11+ VICTIMS)

For the police officers arriving at the house at 12205 Imperial Avenue on 29 October 2009, a detached, three-storey property in a run-down area of East Cleveland, Ohio, it was a pretty routine assignment. A search-and-arrest warrant was out for the home's occupier, 50-year-old Anthony Sowell, on a charge of rape. Although Sowell was known to have served in the US Marine Corps (and had a rap sheet that included 15 years in prison for another sexual assault), the cops in this part of Cleveland were used to handling themselves. And it was not the first time they had come to this property. If Sowell wanted to cause trouble, they would be ready.

There was no response from either front or back door – and

so, following standard procedure, the officers forced their way in, shouted a challenge, and, weapons drawn, began a search for their target.

They would not find Anthony Sowell at home; but instead, something altogether more unexpected ... and horrific.

The first thing they noticed was the smell. Sweet, putrid; like rotting fruit, like ancient eggs, like bad meat. They followed the stench upstairs; by the time they reached the third floor it had become so bad they were gagging.

There, in a room next to what they would later confirm was Sowell's bedroom, lying on the floor, covered in flies, were the badly decomposed remains of two human bodies.

Within days, investigators would find another nine corpses at the property. Some had been buried in shallow graves in the backyard and basement, others were simply stuffed into crawl-spaces around the home.

All were women, all had been strangled, all were bound with a variety of improvised ligatures, including shoelaces, socks, belts, bag straps and electrical cords. Some were naked, others naked only from the waist down. Some of the bodies were intact, others had been dismembered and wrapped in garbage bags and plastic sheets. Most were too decomposed to be identified without medical records. The last of the remains to be discovered was a severed head, left inside a bucket.

On 31 October, two days after police first entered his house, and as children skipped and screamed their way through the streets of East Cleveland dressed as devils and monsters for Halloween, Sowell was caught and arrested, just a mile from his home. A neighbour reported him saying: 'It's all gonna come out. That girl made me do it.'

*

The question that haunts every investigation of a serial killer is: why? What all-consuming compulsion, what terrible impulse or addiction, what emotional need or psychological deficiency drives someone to premeditated, cold-blooded murder – and then to do it again, and again?

In the case of Anthony Sowell, investigating officers were not only horrified by the extent and brutality of the carnage they found inside 12205 Imperial Avenue, but also mystified by the sheer sloppiness of the scene. While attempts had been made to bury some of the bodies, others had just been crammed into whatever spaces could be found around the home. The two victims discovered in the third-floor room were in such an advanced state of decomposition that forensics estimated they might have been there for weeks, and the decapitated head had been left discarded in the bucket, like rubbish.

The callousness of the scene was stunning, but the fact that this was also a place where Sowell was actually living – the third-floor bodies rotting just yards from his own bed – was beyond belief.

The 'whys' were mounting up, and Sowell wasn't about to help answer them. At his trial he made a single statement: 'The only thing I want to say is I'm sorry. I know that might not sound like much, but I am truly sorry from the bottom of my heart.'

Nobody was buying that for an explanation.

*

Anthony Edward Sowell was born on 19 August 1959, and raised in an unconventional family dynamic. His father Thomas was an alcoholic and petty criminal who was rarely – if ever – around; instead, Sowell, along with two of his six siblings, was raised by his mother and grandmother in a Cleveland home just five miles from the scene of his later killings. Also in the house were his seven nieces and nephews, who had moved in after the death of their mother.

Outwardly at least, there were no signs of the monster that Sowell would grow up to become. According to neighbours and teachers interviewed after his arrest, he was a shy, quiet child, polite to adults and, although never running with the popular set, friendly enough to all.

But behind closed doors, Sowell's unusual home circumstances were more bizarre than anyone could have known. The 'shy, friendly' child was already living a double life: a witness to abuse and, before he was a teenager, an abuser himself.

Two of his nieces, twin sisters Ramona and Leona Davis, would claim that Sowell's mother would regularly force them to strip naked in front of the other children, before tying them to a banister and whipping them with electrical cord until they bled. Her own children were not only spared, but even encouraged to watch the assaults.

Worse was to come. According to Leona, when she was 10 years old (and Sowell 11), he began regularly taking her into a bedroom and forcing her to have sex with him. Before long the rapes had become a near-everyday occurrence.

It would take seven long, agonizing years before Leona Davis was free of Anthony Sowell's abuse. On 24 January 1978, aged 18, he entered the United States Marine Corps, having failed to graduate from high school. Rumours had it that he had also got a younger classmate pregnant.

In the Marines Sowell learned to fight, and he learned to kill – and he loved it. The skinny, outwardly shy teenager who reported for boot camp in 1978 would leave the force seven years later a model soldier, in receipt of a Good Conduct Medal and two Letters of Appreciation, as well as a Certificate of Commendation and a rifle sharpshooter award.

If he was a crack shot with a rifle, he also excelled at hand-to-hand and close quarters combat training – learning what the Corps describes as 'basic chokes' and the use of 'basic weapons of opportunity' to subdue and kill a target.

A model soldier Sowell might have been by Marine Corps standards, but once back in East Cleveland, the rot set in. He had returned to the family home, but in the seven years he had been away, the neighbourhood had changed almost unrecognizably. What was previously a comfortable, relatively safe, lower-middle-class area had by the mid-1980s experienced a dramatic and catastrophic decline. A quarter of the population lived below the poverty line, crime rates had rocketed, and once-peaceful streets had become the territory of gangs, prostitutes and junkies.

The prime mover in this social collapse: crack cocaine. The

cheap and chronically addictive drug had, in just a few years, devastated whole communities. By 1985, East Cleveland was a near-wasteland.

Anthony Sowell, the returning US Marine, brandishing his medals and armed with new and deadly abilities, adapted himself to his surroundings immediately. He not only embraced the squalor, but became a part of the culture of fear and lawlessness that had blighted the area.

He began drinking – and drinking heavily. With the drinking came drugs . . . and with the drinking and drug use came violence. Between 1986 and 1989 he racked up an arrest record that included charges of disorderly conduct, driving under the influence, possession of dangerous drugs, public drunkenness, and domestic violence, the last of which saw him sentenced to eight days in jail in 1988.

A decorated serviceman Sowell might have been, but the same twisted urges that had informed his childhood and led him to inflict such hideous abuse on his 10-year-old niece now resurfaced in an even more terrifying manner.

Three women would later claim that they had been sexually assaulted by Sowell in the late 1980s. His modus operandi was simple and effective. Channelling his childhood charm, he would strike up conversations with lone women suffering under the effects of drugs or alcohol, and lure them back to his home on a promise of more of the same. Once inside the house he would force them to strip, choke them, and violently rape them, relying on their fear and mistrust of the police to keep them from reporting the assaults. One would claim that he told her: 'You're my bitch and you had better learn to like it.'

Was Sowell limiting himself only to the threat of killing the women he raped? At the same time that his taste for sexual violence was dangerously escalating, a spate of murders brought another kind of terror to East Cleveland.

Between May 1988 and March 1989, the bodies of three women were found within a mile's radius of Sowell's home – one had been killed in her own house, the others were left dumped in derelict buildings. Two of the victims had been strangled. All of the killings remain unsolved to this day.

On 22 July 1989, Sowell struck again, when he picked up a 21-year-old woman he found wandering the streets. On the pretence of helping her find her boyfriend, he took her home, where he choked and repeatedly raped her – despite her screams that she was three months pregnant – before stuffing a rag in her mouth and binding her wrists and ankles with a tie and a belt. She eventually escaped hours later after he blacked out; and this time Sowell's victim did report the assault to the police.

Sowell's lawyers struck a deal: in exchange for pleading guilty to attempted rape, the other charges (of kidnapping and rape) would be dropped. In September 1990 he was sentenced to 15 years in jail, but was not investigated for the three unsolved murders.

Once again, given structure and discipline, Sowell responded positively. If he had once been a model soldier, he was now a model prisoner. The seriousness of his crime meant he was never recommended for parole, but during his time behind bars he gained his high-school diploma, and passed courses including 'Living Without Violence' and 'Cage Your Rage'. He kicked his addictions to alcohol and drugs, and a psychological evaluation shortly before he was released deemed him unlikely to rape again.

When he finally left prison in June 2005, Anthony Sowell claimed to be a changed man.

He was not.

*

After his release, Sowell did not move back into his childhood home, but instead to 12205 Imperial Avenue, five miles south in the Mount Pleasant district of East Cleveland. And, for a little while at least, he made a stab at living a 'normal' life. He secured a steady job at a local rubber factory, and began a serious relationship with Lori Frazier, niece of Cleveland Mayor Frank Jackson. She moved in with him and although he enjoyed the occasional beer, he remained free of drugs.

In 2007, however, something changed. By late spring the relationship with Frazier had begun to break down, and with it, so did Sowell's brief attempt at clean living. The drinking became heavier, and, perhaps inevitably, led to a return to the drugs that were so easily available on the streets around his home. In July of that year, he lost his job after regularly failing to show up for work, and he signed on for welfare, supplementing his payments by scavenging the streets for scrap metal to sell. What little money he had was inevitably spent getting high.

It was also at this time that another troubled woman disappeared in East Cleveland, two decades after the previous spate of unsolved stranglings.

Crystal Dozier was a 35-year-old mother of seven from Mount Pleasant, and a crack addict for nearly 20 years, who had her first child aged just 13. By 2007 her addiction had become all-consuming – leading all of her children to be taken into care, and to a string of police charges for drug offences and probation violations.

Crack also brought her into Sowell's orbit. The former Marine had become a well-known figure among East Cleveland's addicts – his house was recognized as a regular party venue, with drugs and booze readily available.

In May 2007, Dozier's family reported her missing, but were told that, as she had a history of erratic behaviour, as well as a record for sudden and unexplained prolonged absences, there was little they could do other than wait for her to turn up. She never did.

A month later, an Imperial Avenue resident lodged a complaint with the council; a creeping, noxious smell had seeped into the neighbourhood. The stench of something rotting; the stench of ancient eggs, of bad meat. An investigation was made – and the finger pointed at Ray's Sausage Shop, a family-run factory located next door to Sowell's home.

It would not be until 2009, when police made their horrific discovery at 12205 Imperial Avenue that Crystal Dozier's family finally knew her fate. For two years she had been buried in Sowell's backyard after he had strangled her, the first known victim of a killer who would go on to murder at least another 10 times.

In the meantime, Sowell and Frazier's relationship had finally reached breaking point. She moved out of the house – also complaining of the smell from Ray's Sausage Shop – and with that last remaining vestige of stability removed from his life, Sowell span completely out of control. Now in his late forties, the one-time Marine was a gaunt and near-emaciated alcoholic and drug addict, spending what little money he could scrape together on cheap booze and crack cocaine, prone to sudden bursts of anger and nursing a grievance against his ex-girlfriend that became a bitter hatred of all women.

In June 2008, he claimed his second victim. Tishana Culver was 29, and another casualty of the crack epidemic. Like Crystal Dozier, she had become a mother while still at high school – and like Dozier, her addiction to the drug would lead to her abandoning all six of her children.

Her addiction also led to her selling her body to pay for her habit. It was a practice that led to her death. Told to clean up or get out by her mother, she chose crack. When she disappeared, nobody even reported her missing.

There were 13 months between the murders of Crystal Dozier and Tishana Culver, but over the next five months, Sowell would kill another three times.

Leshanda Long was the youngest of his victims, aged 25 when he lured her to Imperial Avenue on the promise of drugs and alcohol. The mother of three had a wild streak and had spent most of her adult life in and out of detention – when she went missing that August, it barely registered as being unusual for her family. A year later, it would be Leshanda's head that was found in the bucket.

Michelle Mason stood out from Sowell's other victims: although the 45-year-old mother of two had a history of addiction to heroin and cocaine, she had successfully kicked drugs in 2001. By the time of her disappearance in October 2008, she was volunteering at an AIDS charity and living in an apartment close to Imperial Avenue. Interviewed after Sowell's conviction, her sister insisted: 'I don't think she knew him at all. I think he befriended her because he may have spoke nicely to her. She was friendly because she had lived in the streets. She thought she [was a] good judge of people.'

Just one month later, Tonia Carmichael became the fifth body to be buried in 12205 Imperial Avenue. The 52-year-old was Sowell's oldest victim, but fitted his usual modus operandi: chronically addicted to crack, she had lost custody of her children and was reduced to doing whatever it took to secure her next fix. Sowell had strangled and abused her so severely that she could only be identified through DNA technology.

Coincidentally, just days after Carmichael's mother reported her missing, the police picked up Sowell on another charge. Here, finally, was an opportunity to end Sowell's campaign of terror for good, and here, sadly, they missed it.

On 8 December 2008, a bleeding woman ran up to a police car just a few blocks from Imperial Avenue. Shaking with fear, she told them that the ex-Marine had approached her in the street and asked if she wanted to come back to his place to drink beer. When she said no, he punched her, put her in a stranglehold and tried to rip off her clothes. She felt sure that if she hadn't managed to break free, he would have killed her. The cops went to Sowell's home immediately, and arrested him.

And then . . . nothing. Terrified of her attacker, distrusting of the police, the woman changed her mind and refused to file charges. And despite Sowell's previous record, despite the five women who had recently gone missing in the Mount Pleasant district, despite three previous and still unsolved murders by choking in the area, despite the literal stench of death in his street, he was let go.

After his release, perhaps filled with confidence that he would never be caught, that his disastrously addicted targets had fallen so far from conventional society they would either never be missed or, if they escaped, remain too fearful of the police themselves to press charges, he almost immediately killed again.

One murder in 2007. Four killings and a violent assault in 2008. Anthony Sowell was intensifying his taste for violence. Following the classic serial killer pattern, he would keep escalating the horror. In 2009 he murdered six more times, as well as sexually assaulting another two women.

The first of those murders came in January, when 44-year-old Kim Yvette Smith entered 12205 Imperial Avenue to smoke crack cocaine. The only one of Sowell's victims not to have been a mother, she nonetheless fitted his usual pattern: an addict since she was a teenager, her desperate need for the drug had led to a rootless, chaotic life and, at the hands of a man who was determined to act out his violent fantasies in the most horrific way possible, a tragic death.

And still, the stench around Imperial Avenue grew. As more neighbours complained, Ray's Sausage Shop continued to shoulder the blame – the owners spent $20,000 on new plumbing fixtures and sewerage in an attempt to fix the problem. Nothing they could do would make any difference. And the stink of death only increased.

Anthony Sowell would kill five more times – and in April he struck twice in a matter of weeks. Forty-five-year-old grandmother Nancy Cobbs was another addict – but also a supposed friend of Sowell's. The pair would often drink beer together on the porch of her mother's house, a few blocks north of Imperial Avenue, and he was on nodding terms with her family. After her disappearance Sowell professed to be as shocked as everyone else.

Amelda Hunter was another long-term friend. The 47-year-old's life had gone off the rails while she was still a teenager – she had her first baby at 14 years old and became addicted to crack in her twenties. Her family had become used to her disappearing for days at a time when the addiction took hold, and they also knew she was a regular at Sowell's 'open house' at Imperial Avenue. After her disappearance, it was assumed that she was on a drugs binge, and would turn up eventually; again, Sowell claimed no knowledge of her whereabouts.

The same month, another friend, Tanja Doss, claimed that he had slapped, choked and sexually assaulted her after running out of crack. She curled up on the bed and, miraculously, this time he calmed down.

By now, the killings had become routine to Sowell – and followed a predictable pattern. Two more women with chronic drug addictions, anarchic home lives and a history of petty crime would be murdered in June: Janice Webb, 48, and Telacia Fortson, 31, were picked up in the same way as his other victims; and, as with those other victims, their sudden disappearances attracted little official interest or attention. In the case of Fortson, her mother did not even report her missing until the bodies began turning up.

Sowell's last kill, 48-year-old Diane Turner, whom he beat and strangled to death, was to be one of the corpses that police found rotting in the third-floor room next to his bedroom. Between 1991 and 2009 she had been arrested a dozen times on drug charges, and was a familiar figure to the Mount Pleasant cops as a prostitute, flagging down cars, desperate for cash for her next fix. She had gone to Sowell's home in September 2009, either in search of crack, or to smoke it. She did not leave again alive.

Turner may have been well known to East Cleveland police, but so broken were her family relationships that it took an entire month before any relatives could be found to match DNA with her remains. She was the last of Sowell's 11 confirmed victims to be identified.

Days later, Sowell struck one last time – persuading another woman to come back to Imperial Avenue to drink liquor. Almost as soon as she entered the house he attacked her, choking her with an extension cord and raping her until she passed out. When she recovered consciousness, he let her go on condition that she return with $50.

She did not return, and on 27 October, she went to the police. Two days after that detectives entered 12205 Imperial Avenue and the full depth of Anthony Sowell's depravity began to be revealed.

*

The whys of Sowell's journey from victim of abuse to abuser, alcoholic, drug addict, rapist and finally murderer remain the subject of conjecture, even a decade or more after his conviction. Was his rage kindled by the abuse he witnessed as a child? Was it later inflamed by the collapse of his relationship with Lori Frazier – hence his chilling statement: 'that girl made me do it'? Was he punishing the women he felt were demeaning themselves by selling their bodies to pay for drugs? Was he, in some twisted way, himself a victim of the crack epidemic that reduced its users to their basest instincts and made casual brutality and degradation a part of everyday life for addicts?

The whys will remain a mystery. On 22 July 2011, Anthony Sowell was convicted of the murders of all 11 women found in 12205 Imperial Avenue, and on 14 September he was sentenced to death. He would remain on death row for another 10 years, before dying in prison of a terminal illness.

In December 2011, 12205 Imperial Avenue was demolished. It stays a vacant lot to this day.

Ray's Sausage Shop remains open.

2

JOHN WAYNE GACY

(USA, 1972–8, 33 VICTIMS)

They called him the Killer Clown.

A decade before Stephen King created Pennywise the clown in his 1986 horror novel *It*, a real-life children's entertainer was terrorizing Chicago, Illinois. Over six years he raped, tortured and murdered dozens of young men and boys between the ages of 14 and 21, stashing their bodies in the crawl space beneath his single-storey, two-bedroom ranch-style house in the quiet suburban community of Norwood Park, close to Chicago's O'Hare Airport. After his twenty-ninth slaying, he ran out of space to bury the bodies and began throwing them into the Des Plaines River.

His performing alter-ego was Pogo the Clown. His real name

was John Wayne Gacy, and he was perhaps the most terrifying of serial killer types: that of the monster hiding in plain sight.

'I always tell people that the scary thing about Gacy was that he wasn't scary at all,' his lawyer Sam Amirante said. 'That's the scary thing – he could have been anyone's brother or father, uncle.'

The paunchy, affable thirty-something was a supposed pillar of the community: a respected member of local political and youth mentoring groups, a beloved amateur magician who would entertain sick children at local hospitals, a popular and generous neighbour and host of huge annual summer parties attended by up to 300 friends and colleagues, and a keen, hardworking entrepreneur who had built up several businesses from scratch and was known to help young men into steady work.

Hidden from all those friends, colleagues, neighbours and admirers was Gacy's real passion: the deliberate, planned, sadistic torture, sexual assault and murder of those same young men he professed to help. So prolonged and brutal were the agonies he inflicted upon his victims that he later claimed several of them had begged for death.

'I'm getting round to it,' he would reply, and resume the torment.

In 1980 he was convicted of 33 murders; at the time, it was the most for any single person in US history. He never showed any remorse.

'When they paint this image that I was this monster who picked up these altar boys along the streets and swatted them like flies, I said, "This is ludicrous,"' he claimed after his conviction. 'If you believe you've lived your life the right way, then you do not have nothing [sic] to fear.'

*

John Wayne Gacy may have been one of the most prolific and most sadistic serial killers of the twentieth century, but the first time he took a life was not a premeditated attack.

At around 11pm on 2 January 1972, a Greyhound bus rolled into the dark, deserted, freezing terminal in Chicago and a tall, blond, softly spoken boy disembarked. Sixteen-year-old Timothy McCoy had spent Christmas with his cousins in Eaton Rapids, Michigan, and was travelling the 650 miles back to his father's home in Nebraska alone. The journey meant a change at Chicago, but once in the city, McCoy found his connecting bus would not be leaving until midday the following day.

There was no option but to wrap his coat a little tighter, find a quiet spot in the terminal, and see out the 13 hours as best he could. Perhaps once it got light he could walk around the city a little, see the sights.

He had barely settled onto a bench when a friendly voice surprised him. 'Are you okay?' the man asked. 'Have you got nowhere to stay?'

McCoy may only have been 16 years old, but he was not naïve. He knew the dangers of the big city – and of the kinds of men you might find hanging around a bus terminal at midnight. He eyed the man warily: he looked around 30 years old, was short, a little overweight, dressed like a square . . . and he had a kind face, a friendly voice. He did not seem a threat, and anyway, if it came to it, McCoy decided, he was pretty confident he could handle anything this guy might try on.

The man explained that he suffered from insomnia – and that on nights when he couldn't sleep he liked to drive around the deserted city streets, see the lights of downtown Chicago free from the daytime crowds and noise. He had been passing the bus station when he saw McCoy; he was a divorced father of two, he missed his kids, and his fatherly instinct meant he was immediately concerned for the boy. This was not the safest area, so he thought he should check to see if he could help in any way.

Perhaps McCoy was naïve after all, or perhaps he was disarmed by the calm, easy-going demeanour of the man. Either way, he accepted the offer to join him on a nocturnal sightseeing trip of the city: it had to be better than bedding down on a bench in the draughty bus station – and at least it would pass a few hours before dawn.

Once in the car, McCoy's defences dropped still further. The man introduced himself as John Gacy, he was charming and funny, and after a couple of hours zigzagging through Chicago's empty streets, when he suggested that McCoy crash in the spare room of his house before getting a lift back to the Greyhound station in the morning, the young man accepted.

What happened over the next few hours remains uncertain. Was the offer really simply of a bed for the night, or did Gacy expect more? Did he take more, with or without Timothy

McCoy's consent? Whatever the truth, we only have Gacy's own account of the following morning for any clue as to why, six years later, McCoy's remains would be found rotting under his floorboards.

According to a prison interview, Gacy said he woke on 3 January to find McCoy standing over his bed with a kitchen knife in his hand. Panicked, he jumped up and made a lunge for the blade; McCoy raised his hands – in self-defence, or in surrender – and in doing so slashed Gacy's arm.

The older man saw red. 'Motherfucker! I'll kill you!' he screamed, and suddenly possessed of a strength and rage that McCoy could never have guessed at, laid into him, kicking, punching, slamming him to the floor. Before McCoy could react he was prone, Gacy straddling him, and then the knife was in Gacy's grip and he was stabbing, stabbing, into the young man's chest, twisting and gouging the blade with ever greater ferocity. As blood filled the boy's lungs and his spasms grew weaker, Gacy finally got up, and went into the kitchen to wash the blade clean.

And that's when he saw the table. It was set for two; by the cooker there was a carton of eggs and a slab of unsliced bacon. Timothy McCoy had not come into Gacy's bedroom with the intention of killing him, he had come to tell him he was cooking breakfast – he just happened to be still carrying the bacon knife.

Was Gacy filled with remorse at this terrible, tragic misunderstanding? On the contrary. In his prison interview, he said that listening to McCoy's desperate final moments, his 'gurgulations' and spasmodic gasps for air, had been the most intense sexual experience of his life. 'That's when I realized that death was the ultimate thrill,' he said.

Once McCoy was definitively dead, he carried the teenager's body into the crawl space beneath the house and buried him in a shallow grave. And for over half a decade he never gave another thought to the boy who was just trying to get home to his father.

Timothy McCoy had given John Wayne Gacy a taste of the 'ultimate thrill'. He may have been his first murder victim . . . but he was not the first boy to have been abused by the Killer Clown.

*

A charming, charismatic man Gacy may have seemed outwardly, but the moral deficiencies that would become all-consuming in adulthood had their roots in his upbringing, and took a grip in his adolescence.

Though Gacy had been born into an outwardly 'normal' family in Chicago in March 1942, his relationship with his father was nonetheless strained from the start. The head of the family was an alcoholic and a bully, who would mock his son's close relationship to his mother and two sisters and declare him a 'sissy' for his lack of interest in sports; occasionally the abuse would become physical, as he beat the boy with a leather belt. When a childhood accident meant that Gacy developed a heart condition and began to suffer blackouts, his father accused him of faking the illness, even as he lay in hospital.

The effect of this on Gacy's developing psyche was complicated. Far from turning him against his father, a kind of Stockholm syndrome developed in which he became desperate to gain the love and approval of the man who was so cruel to him.

The first outward sign that there were other psychological issues came in 1962, when he was 20. That April he finally found the courage to escape his father, and he fled to Las Vegas, where he secured a job as a mortuary attendant and occasional pallbearer. Dead bodies held no fear for him – to save money he even slept on a cot behind the embalming room. It was here that what would become the two dominating factors of Gacy's life came together. One evening, he crept into the coffin of a teenager whose death had left him with a permanent erection: Gacy fondled the corpse, before arranging himself beneath it. Sex and death had become entwined.

After a few months, Gacy returned to Chicago, where he at least tried to settle down into the kind of life his father might approve of. He enrolled in business college before managing a shoe company and joining the local chapter of a civic and leadership organization known as the Jaycees. He also met and married his first wife, Marlynn Myers; the couple moved to the town of Waterloo, Iowa, in 1964 and their two children were born a few years later.

In Waterloo, Gacy appeared to be living a model life. The loving husband and father took charge of a successful Kentucky Fried Chicken franchise, and again had taken up with the local Jaycees: in 1967 he served on the Waterloo chapter board of directors and was named 'outstanding Vice

President' of the association. His generosity, work ethic and willingness to go the extra mile to help others made him a popular member of the community, and he even acquired the nickname 'Colonel' thanks to his habit of bringing free fried chicken to Jaycees meetings.

It was all a lie. Gacy's perfect life was nothing more than a whited sepulchre, and beneath the flawless façade there was deep corruption.

Unknown to Marlynn, Gacy had been experimenting with his sexuality, and had found his taste ran along very particular lines: specifically that of teenage boys. Throughout 1967 and early 1968, dozens of teenagers would be enticed back to his house on the promise of watching pornographic movies; once there they were plied with alcohol before being sexually assaulted. Some were paid $50 to keep quiet, others intimidated into silence. One boy, 15-year-old Donald Vorhees, the son of a fellow Jaycee, was told: 'You have to have sex with a man before you start having sex with women.'

In March 1968, Vorhees reported the assault to his father, and Gacy was arrested. Before the case could come to trial, Vorhees was badly beaten up by another teenager – when police tracked the attacker down, he admitted that Gacy had promised to pay off his $300 car loan in return for intimidating Vorhees to drop the charge.

On 3 December, John Wayne Gacy was convicted of sodomy and sentenced to 10 years in prison. The same day, Marlynn Myers petitioned for divorce. He would not see her or his two children again.

*

Gacy served just 18 months of his sentence before being released on parole, and once free, he repeated the trick he had pulled off after his return from Las Vegas.

Back in Chicago, he secured work as a chef, and supplemented his income as a jobbing painter and renovator. He found he had a talent not only for renovation, but also for business – before long the kitchen work was dropped, and he launched PDM Contractors (for 'painting, decorating and maintenance') and moved into a larger house, on West Summerdale Avenue, Norwood Park.

He also pursued his other, secret sideline.

In February 1971, a teenage boy told police that Gacy had approached him at Chicago's Greyhound bus terminal and, after convincing him to accept a lift, had driven him to his home and attempted to force him to have sex. Gacy was arrested for assault but the charges were dropped after the boy failed to show up to testify. Astonishingly, the parole board in Iowa were not told of the arrest, and Gacy remained a free man. Less than a year later, he used the same technique to pick up Timothy McCoy, with fatal consequences.

But if John Wayne Gacy's first victim was a tragic accident, the 32 that followed were wholly deliberate.

Six months after he had buried McCoy's lifeless body in the crawl space beneath his house, Gacy married again, to childhood friend Carole Hoff. And with Carole at his side he once again developed the persona of happy family man, joining

Chicago civic and mentoring groups, volunteering for the local Democrat Party and building PDM Contractors into a large and successful business.

He also joined the 'Jolly Joker' clown club, creating the character of Pogo the Clown, complete with voluminous red-and-white striped outfit and full face paint, including a garish, outsized, scarlet red mouth. As Pogo he would perform at parties, charity events and fundraisers, as well as for sick children at Chicago hospitals. The act would involve the usual mime and pratfalls, but also rudimentary magic tricks.

Part of the success of PDM, he claimed, was his practice of employing teenage boys to carry out basic labouring work: not only were they were cheaper to pay and keen to impress, but by providing them with steady employment he adopted a mentor-like persona, giving the boys opportunities while helping them to contribute to their community too.

Gacy's real motivations were not so pure – and his secret activities were escalating. By 1973 he told Carole that the garage was to be his dedicated workshop, and was strictly out of bounds to her. Most evenings he would be gone on 'site visits' or to see 'potential clients' before returning to the garage, where he would 'work' until deep into the night.

In reality, Gacy was cruising for underage sex. Runaways and lone travellers would be picked up at the bus station or on the street with the promise of warmth and a bed for the night, kids were lured into his car thanks to a makeshift flashing siren and a false police badge, and potential teenage employees enticed into the garage to discuss just what their role at PDM might involve.

By 1975, Carole no longer believed his stories. Not only had she seen him bringing a trail of boys into his supposed workshop, but she had also discovered his stash of gay pornography – some of which included images of young men covered in blood. Additionally, the house had begun to stink – a problem with drainage from a broken sewage pipe, Gacy insisted – and no matter how much lime or concrete he poured into the crawl space, nothing seemed to shift it.

In early 1976, she moved out, and in March their divorce was finalized. By then Gacy had already killed another two times.

The first of these bodies remains unidentified. Most likely another runaway whom he had picked up and brought to the garage for sex, the boy, who forensics later estimated to be between 14 and 18 years old, had been strangled, and buried beside Timothy McCoy beneath the house.

On 31 July 1975, Gacy struck again – and this time he looked closer to home.

Eighteen-year-old John Butkovich was a PDM employee; he had previously argued with Gacy over several weeks' pay he was owed, and with Carole away for the evening, Gacy invited him over to his garage to discuss the issue.

Once they were inside, Gacy opened a six pack and assured Butkovich that they could settle the dispute amicably. He was an easy-going, tolerant boss, friendly with the boys who worked for him, and before long the argument was forgotten as the two enjoyed a drink and a laugh. That was when Gacy produced a pair of handcuffs and asked Butkovich if he wanted to see Pogo the Clown perform a magic trick.

'Sure,' said the teenager, and Gacy turned around with his hands behind his back and asked Butkovich to cuff him. Once secured, he turned around again, manipulated the lock with the key he had hidden between his fingers, and hey presto! His wrists were free and the cuffs were off.

Now it was Butkovich's turn to be cuffed – with a promise that he would learn how to do the trick himself.

Once the boy was manacled, however, Gacy's demeanour changed dramatically. The friendly smile had become a sneer, the voice turned hard. 'The trick is, you have to have the key,' he whispered, and pushed Butkovich to the floor, where he bound his legs.

From that point the young man didn't stand a chance. Gacy raped and tortured him for hours, before finally sitting on his chest. Now, he told Butkovich, it's time for the rope trick.

A knotted tourniquet was produced, and a hammer handle looped through. It was placed over his head and with every turn of the handle the rope grew agonizingly tighter. The last words Butkovich heard before he died were the grim reassurance: 'This is the last trick.'

Once his body had stopped convulsing, it joined the other two, and more lime and concrete were ordered.

After his split from Carole, Gacy took advantage of his new-found freedom to expand his lust for murder to unimaginable levels. Between April and December 1976 he killed 15 times, abducting the first of these victims, 18-year-old Darrell Samson, just one month after his divorce was finalized. One month after that, on 14 May, he snatched 15-year-old Randall

Reffett and 14-year-old Samuel Stapleton as they walked home, and killed them both together in what he subsequently called a 'double'.

He struck another five times between June and August, five times again before the end of October, and twice in December.

And still, despite the slaughter, nobody in Norwood Park was any the wiser. It was also at this time that he hosted several huge themed barbecue parties for the local community. Hundreds of guests in fancy dress, including friends, neighbours, clients, employees, and Jaycees and Democrat representatives would drink beer and enjoy hot dogs and burgers just yards from the mass grave he was accumulating in his cellar.

All but two of his victims that year were kids he found on the streets, Gacy using the methods he had honed as he cruised for sex the years before: either picked up, like Timothy McCoy, at bus stations or offered a lift home, or else tricked into believing Gacy was an undercover cop. Once they were inside the car, Gacy no longer bothered trying to charm them back to his house – before they knew what had happened, a chloroform-soaked rag would be pressed against their face; when they regained consciousness they were already bound and helpless on the floor of his garage.

Gacy's other two victims that year were PDM employees. William Bundy, a 19-year-old whose last contact with his parents was to tell them he was going to a party, was killed by suffocation: he died with a rag stuffed in his mouth and was buried beneath the master bedroom. Gregory Godzik was just 17 when he disappeared from outside his girlfriend's house.

He had previously talked of how much he enjoyed working for PDM, even helping Gacy out with odd jobs around his boss's house. Gacy later said that one of those jobs had been to dig the same trench in which he would later be buried.

The carnage continued unabated throughout the following year. In 1977 another nine bodies were added to the mass grave. All were young men between the ages of 16 and 21, all suffered horrific sexual abuse before they died. Some were killed with the rope trick, others had rags forced deep down their throats, suffocating them or else forcing them to choke on their own vomit. Many had been tortured for hours – a particular favourite being to drag them into the bathroom and repeatedly force their heads under the water in a primitive form of the technique known as 'waterboarding'. If a victim should pass out, Gacy would revive them in order to continue the horror properly.

On 30 December, he tried the same trick with a 19-year-old called Robert Donnelly, whom he abducted from a bus stop at gunpoint. For once, however, he did not see the job through to the end but instead drove him back to Chicago and released him. Donnelly reported the assault to the police, but when questioned the older man claimed the two had consensual 'slave sex' – and that Donnelly's grievance came from Gacy's refusal to pay him. The police believed Gacy's story, and the case was dropped.

Three months later, on 21 March 1978, Gacy once again spared one of his victims. Jeffrey Rignall – who at 26 was by far the oldest of his targets – told police that Gacy had chloroformed him, locked his hands and feet onto beams of wood, and subjected him to hours of torture with candles, whips and sex toys, before dumping him in Lincoln Park, in the north of the city.

This time the cops did take Gacy's accuser seriously, and he was arrested on 15 July on a charge of assault and battery, and released on bail.

By that time, Gacy had added another two kills to his tally – and so prolific had been his murder spree that he had run out of space to store the bodies. His thirtieth victim, Timothy O'Rourke, had instead been thrown from a bridge into the Des Plaines River. Another three would follow in November and December – and it would be the last of these that would finally bring an end to Gacy's three-year frenzy of killing.

*

When 15-year-old Robert Piest went missing on 11 December, it did not take long for the police to knock on Gacy's door. The teenager had been working at a pharmacy in Des Plaines that Gacy had visited that afternoon – and his last contact before he disappeared was to tell his mother that 'some contractor wants to talk to me about a job'. He was last seen wearing a blue parka jacket at 9pm. By 10pm he was dead.

This time the police did their job properly. As the suspected 'contractor' Piest had gone to see that night, Gacy was the first step in their investigation. When a background check revealed that he had an assault and battery charge outstanding, as well as a previous conviction for the sodomy of a 15-year-old boy, they called him in for questioning, as well as obtaining a search warrant for his home.

Gacy denied everything, but the search was incriminating. Handcuffs, sex toys and violent pornography were found, as well as several lengths of rope and a metre-long length of wood with holes drilled into each end. Also present was children's underwear, and a blue parka jacket in a size too small to fit Gacy.

But it was a visit to the bathroom that made the detectives' blood run cold. As one of the investigators washed his hands, a hot-air furnace kicked into life – and the sudden blast of air that came through the vent from the crawl space smelled terrible. It took a moment for the cop to realize just how terrible.

It smelled like the city morgue. It smelled like death.

A week later, John Wayne Gacy confessed to the murder of Robert Piest and what he casually dismissed as 'around 30' others. Over the following three months, a painstaking search uncovered 29 bodies beneath his house, as well as four more washed up in the Des Plaines River. It was slaughter on a scale not seen before – and when the details of the terrors inflicted on his victims began to emerge, it revealed an evil that seemed beyond belief.

On 12 March 1980, Gacy was found guilty of 33 counts of murder, the most by any individual in US history. The following day the same jury took a little over two hours to impose the death penalty.

Gacy would spend 14 years on death row, before finally

being executed by lethal injection in May 1994. In that time his notoriety almost eclipsed the horrors of his actions; the Killer Clown had become a symbol for a certain kind of rottenness lurking beneath the veneer of the American Dream. He was the monster among us, the suburban killer hiding in plain sight, the serial killer next door.

It took until 1986 before Timothy McCoy was properly identified – until then his body had been known simply as 'Greyhound Bus Boy'. Another five of the 33 young men and boys John Wayne Gacy killed remain unidentified, nearly five decades after they died.

3

DENNIS NILSEN

(UK, 1978–83, 15 VICTIMS)

At almost exactly the same time that detectives began to uncover the scale and brutality of John Wayne Gacy's crimes, 4,000 miles away, in London, another serial killer was beginning his own murder campaign.

The parallels between the grisly careers of John Wayne Gacy and Dennis Nilsen are uncanny; both sought out young men whom they would bring home for sex, before killing them and stowing their bodies in their homes. But at the same time they were worlds apart.

The horrors perpetrated by the American entrepreneur and the British civil servant were separately shot through with characteristics wholly peculiar to the circumstances in which they lived, worked and killed. If the clown costumes and barbecue parties that formed the backdrop to Gacy's murders were symbolic of the dynamism and extravagance of 1970s America, then Nilsen's altogether greyer, more drab existence summed up late 1970s and early 1980s Britain just as succinctly.

It even extends to the way they killed. Gacy's murders were loud, messy, physical affairs, full of threats and taunts and extended periods of torture; Nilsen's were cold, dispassionate, almost devoid of emotion altogether. And, most chillingly, the real business only began after the death of his victims.

The press called the winter of 1978-9 'the winter of discontent'. They had no idea just how ugly it would get.

*

In late 1978, Dennis Nilsen was a lonely, awkward, unhappy man. Employed as a supervisor in a central London job centre, his days were long and tedious; the nights, drinking whisky and lager in his north London flat, even more so. The former soldier and policeman lived alone, was estranged from his family, had no real friends, and, though he had known he was gay since he was a teenager, at the age of 33 was still not fully comfortable with his sexuality, and had never enjoyed a serious relationship.

The period between Christmas and New Year was especially difficult. The job centre was shut, the weather was bitter, and the forced jollity of the festive decorations he saw through every window and in every shopfront only depressed him further. There wasn't even anyone he could give a Christmas gift to, or expect one from.

By 30 December Nilsen was in a deep gloom. He spent that day in his living room with the curtains drawn, staring at the walls, listening to music, drinking spirits and feeling sorry for himself. By the evening he'd reached breaking point. He had to get out of the flat, seek some kind of human company.

In the Cricklewood Arms pub, his mood did not improve until his attention was caught by an altercation at the bar. A young man had been refused service, despite insisting he was 18 and legally allowed to drink alcohol. The barman shrugged, the man stormed out, and after a moment, Nilsen followed him.

His name was Stephen Holmes, and he was not 18, but 14. After expressing his sympathies, Nilsen mentioned he had plenty of alcohol back at his flat. The boy barely hesitated before following him home.

Once inside, the pair spent the evening drinking themselves into a stupor, before crawling into bed together. Nilsen fell asleep with a smile on his face. Those few hours may have been the happiest the lonely 33-year-old had felt in years.

The next morning, Nilsen woke first. As he gazed at the sleeping boy, he felt the happiness of the previous evening drain away, replaced by a terrible sense of loss. '[I was] afraid to wake him in case he left me,' he later confessed. '[He was] to stay with me over the New Year whether he wanted to or not.'

Carefully, quietly, so as not to wake Holmes and spoil the tranquillity of the moment, Nilsen reached into the pile of discarded clothes on the floor and retrieved his necktie. With the utmost care he looped it gently around the boy's neck, before straddling him and pulling it as tight as he could.

Holmes immediately jerked awake and fought back. As the pair rolled off the bed and along the floor, Nilsen kept a grip on the tie, choking ever harder, pushing him against the wall as he throttled him from behind.

Finally, the struggles got weaker, until the young body went limp. But the job was not yet done; Holmes, though unconscious, still breathed. Cursing, Nilsen ran into the kitchen and filled a plastic bucket with water. Gripping his hair, he thrust Holmes's head into the water and held it there.

'After a few minutes the bubbles stopped coming,' he later remembered. 'I lifted him up and sat him on the armchair. The water was dripping from his short, brown, curly hair.'

After recovering with a cup of coffee and a cigarette, Nilsen carried the body into his bathroom, where he gently washed it all over, before placing him back on the bed. A little while after that, he put the corpse under the floorboards. Stephen Holmes was staying after all.

*

Dennis Nilsen kept Holmes's body for another eight months, periodically bringing it out from under the floorboards, washing it, applying make-up to cover the more obvious signs of putrefaction, and caressing or even sleeping beside it.

He was the first person killed by Dennis Nilsen. Over the following five years, another 14 would follow, without anyone ever suspecting a thing. Only eight of Nilsen's victims have ever been identified, and of those, only three (including Holmes) had a permanent address at the time of their murder.

Nilsen targeted the lonely and lost boys of London – perhaps because they were less likely to be missed – or perhaps because he saw something of himself in them.

Born on 23 November 1945 in Aberdeenshire, Scotland, Dennis Andrew Nilsen barely knew his father, a Norwegian soldier who left when he was just three. He was a quiet child, most comfortable in the presence of his maternal grandfather, who worked on the fishing boats from Fraserburgh, north of Aberdeen. When his grandfather was not out at sea fishing, the pair would often go for long walks in the wild Scottish countryside.

When Nilsen was just six, however, his grandfather died while out at sea: the boy took it hard, and withdrew from his mother and siblings. By the time he was a teenager his sense of isolation grew still more acute, as he struggled with the realization that he was gay. Homosexuality would remain illegal in Britain until 1967 – for the confused, withdrawn adolescent, the knowledge that his emerging identity made him technically a criminal was devastating.

After school, Nilsen sought refuge in the army, serving until 1972 and becoming a cook, where he learned basic butchery. While stationed in West Berlin, he had his first sexual experience, with a female prostitute. He later said he found the act 'depressing'.

By the time he left the forces, homosexuality was no longer

illegal, but attitudes – especially in the closed communities of rural Scotland – had not changed. After his older brother Olav scorned him for his sexuality, and then told their strictly conservative mother that Dennis was gay, Nilsen left Scotland altogether to join the police force in London. He would never speak to Olav again, and relations with his mother and younger sister were reduced to the bare minimum.

The police force did not suit Nilsen – not least because once in the capital he began experimenting further, becoming a regular at gay pubs. Still he found no solace in sex, later describing the liaisons as 'soul destroying', and a 'vain search for inner peace'.

One year after completing his police training, Nilsen quit, and took a pen-pushing position in a job centre. A year after that, in November 1975, he moved into the ground-floor flat at 195 Melrose Avenue in the drab north London suburb of Cricklewood. As part of his tenancy agreement, he had exclusive use of the rear garden.

For three years he sank deeper into a dull and depressing routine: commuting to central London every morning, spending the day conscientiously but quietly behind his desk, barely interacting with his colleagues, never socializing with them, before making the journey home again to spend the evenings alone, but for a bottle of whisky and his record player. When he did venture out to the pub, he sat by himself. Those who knew him did not exactly dislike him – they were bored by him. He was a bored, and a boring, man.

Outwardly, nothing changed after 30 December 1978.

But as the months passed, behind the closed door and shut windows of his flat in Melrose Avenue, Stephen Holmes was beginning to become a problem. Throughout the spring and summer of 1979 he remained under Nilsen's floorboards, but as the weather grew warmer, the body began to decay irretrievably. Nilsen still brought him out for regular bathings, but by August it had become clear that their time together was over.

On 11 August, Nilsen ended it for good. Building a bonfire at the far end of his garden, he dragged Holmes's body out after dark, struck a match, and burned the corpse. Afterwards he cleaned the flat thoroughly, spraying deodorant and insecticide into the space beneath the floor, erasing the last evidence that the boy had ever existed at all.

For nearly four months, Dennis Nilsen resumed his quiet, dull life, but as Christmas once again approached, the unbearable loneliness returned. He needed a new housemate, a new lover.

On 3 December, Nilsen spent his lunch break in a pub close to his work. Also enjoying a drink there was 23-year-old Canadian tourist Kenneth Ockenden. The two struck up a conversation, and, unusually, the Canadian did not seem as bored by Nilsen's chatter as everyone else. The older man's mood brightened and he offered to take him sightseeing for the rest of the afternoon, before returning to Cricklewood for dinner and more drinks.

It was on the way back to Melrose Avenue that Ockenden mentioned this was to be his last night in London: his flight home was scheduled the very next day.

Once again, Nilsen was to lose someone he had only just met. Once again, the thought was intolerable.

As the pair sat in his flat, listening to music, Nilsen strangled Ockenden with the cord from his headphones, twisting and dragging him across the floor until he was dead. He then poured himself another drink, closed his eyes and enjoyed the rest of the record.

Ockenden was then stripped and bathed and laid on the bed, and Nilsen climbed in beside him, killer and corpse sleeping together naked like lovers. In the morning Ockenden was stuffed into a wardrobe, and Nilsen caught his usual bus to work.

For five months, Nilsen and Ockenden lived together in a ghoulish version of domestic bliss. By day the Canadian would 'sleep' beneath the floorboards; every few nights Nilsen would bring him out for bathing before sitting him in an armchair, where the two would 'watch' television together, Nilsen talking to him as if he were alive. He also bought a Polaroid camera and took several pictures of the dead body in poses around the flat: happy snaps for the Nilsen family album.

Naturally, it could not last: it was not long before Ockenden's body too began to suffer the inevitable decay, and the cosy nights watching TV together had to come to an end. From then on, Ockenden stayed sleeping under the floor.

On 17 May Nilsen struck again, in what now seems to be the last of what might be called his 'relationship' killings.

Martyn Duffy was a 16-year-old runaway, who Nilsen encountered sleeping rough at Euston train station. He was lured back to the flat with the promise of a meal and a bed for the evening and, initially at least, Nilsen was as good as his word. The two ate dinner, drank a couple of beers each, and Duffy fell asleep on the bed. He woke with a ligature around his neck and Nilsen straddling him, pinning his arms down with his legs.

As with Holmes, strangulation itself was not enough; Nilsen carried the limp body to the kitchen, filled the sink, and held the boy's head under until the bubbles stopped. He then ran a bath for the pair of them before returning to bed – together this time. 'I talked to him,' Nilsen later said, 'and mentioned that his body was the youngest looking I had ever seen.'

The teenager spent two weeks in the wardrobe, before joining the rotting remains of Ockenden under the floorboards.

There had been nearly a year between the murders of Stephen Holmes and Kenneth Ockenden, and then five months between Ockenden and Duffy. After his next victim, 27-year-old male prostitute Billy Sutherland, whom he met in late August 1980 and later confessed that he could not even remember killing – stating only that in the morning, there was 'another dead body' – he would kill another eight times in just 12 months.

All were runaways, male prostitutes, or young men he met in pubs and convinced to come back to Melrose Avenue to continue drinking. All were strangled, bathed, and added to the pile of bodies under his floorboards, with some occasionally brought out to spend the night in bed with him. Seven of those victims remain unidentified.

Nilsen was no longer killing in a twisted search for a lasting relationship – he was doing so because killing young men was simply what he did. There was little in the way of rage or desperation behind the slayings; they were a cold, composed, almost disinterested exercise in control. If Dennis Nilsen was a boring man, then the tedium of his life even extended to his identity as a serial killer.

This was most striking in the way he approached the problem of getting rid of the bodies once he ran out of space beneath his floorboards, or the stench and swarms of flies threatened to attract the attention of his neighbours. If the murders themselves were terrifyingly emotionless, then Nilsen's subsequent disposal of the corpses is horrifying almost beyond comprehension.

First the bodies would be brought into the kitchen and laid on the stone floor. Then, stripped to his underwear, Nilsen would carefully dissect them, removing their organs and placing them in a plastic bag. Arms and legs would be severed with a kitchen knife, heads cut off and boiled in a specially bought large pot. Limbs would be kept in bags in the garden shed, the torsos stuffed in suitcases.

The luggage would then be placed into a bonfire at the bottom of the garden, with an old car tyre thrown on top to disguise the smell of burning flesh. While the fire burned, he would empty the bags of dissected organs into a gap in his fence for animals to eat. After the fire cooled, the ashes were raked into the ground – on one occasion he discovered a whole skull still intact, and had to smash it up with a rake.

Six bodies would be dissected, dismembered and burned this way in late 1980; another five would follow in a bonfire before Nilsen left Melrose Avenue in October the following year. After his eventual arrest, police would find over 1,000 bone fragments in the garden.

Dennis Nilsen's final victim at Melrose Avenue was 23-year-old Malcolm Barlow, an orphan with mental health problems whom he had initially found collapsed outside his flat. Nilsen had called him an ambulance but after being released from hospital, on 18 September 1981, Barlow returned to say thanks. He would not escape a second time: after drinking rum and falling asleep on the sofa, he was strangled, for no other reason, Nilsen later said, than because he found Barlow's presence a nuisance.

*

One month later, after being told by his landlord that he wanted to renovate 195 Melrose Avenue, Dennis Nilsen moved into a new property, in nearby Cranley Gardens. This time he was in the attic flat, one of six in the building, and as a result he had no access to the garden, nor space underneath the floorboards. It slowed down his killing spree, but by no means stopped it.

The first man to be murdered at 23D Cranley Gardens was John Howlett, a 23-year-old who he had met once before in the pub. Their second encounter, in March 1982, was to end with Howlett returning to Nilsen's flat to continue drinking, before he eventually fell asleep on the bed.

Did Nilsen bring Howlett home with the intention of killing him? It seems by no means certain. The fact that he had not killed since September of the year before, plus the circumstances of his new flat meaning that getting rid of any bodies would be so much harder, seems to suggest that he had considered halting – or at least putting on hold – the murders... until Howlett apparently made up his mind for him.

Nilsen did not want the man to spend the night in his flat, and asked him to leave several times. When Howlett ignored those requests and instead got into his bed, Nilsen lost his temper. Grabbing a loose upholstery strap, he wrapped it around Howlett's neck and pulled hard.

Howlett fought back; Nilsen twisted harder. The struggle continued across the room, until Howlett struck his head and fell unconscious. Nilsen kept the strap tight around the younger man's neck, squeezing with all his strength – but still he would not die. Eventually, he was dragged into the bathroom, held under the water until drowned, and then left slumped in the bath for the rest of the night.

In the morning, Dennis Nilsen woke to a problem. What was he to do with the body? For the moment he stuffed it into a closet and went to work.

By the time he got home that evening, he'd arrived at a solution. With nowhere to keep the corpse and a bonfire out of the question, he instead dissected and removed the organs as usual, before filleting the whole body into small chunks of meat. The head, hands and feet, along with some larger pieces, were boiled, the rest of the flesh and the organs chopped up and flushed down the toilet. Most of the bones were put into his rubbish bin, the larger ones he hurled over a fence into waste ground.

If Nilsen the murderer was back, then Nilsen the ruthless, methodical desecrator of his victims' bodies was not only also back, but had descended into new depths of depravity.

He later claimed he did not even remember killing his next victim, Archibald Allan, a 27-year-old who he had met while hailing a cab in central London in September 1982. According to Nilsen, Allan had choked on an omelette in his kitchen: the subsequent forensic analysis of the remains of his neck bones suggested that instead he had been strangled as he ate. He too had a cooling-off period in the bath before being dissected, filleted and flushed down the toilet in the same way as Howlett.

Nilsen's final victim was 20-year-old homeless drug addict Steven Sinclair. Luring him back to Cranley Gardens on 23 January 1983, as a safe place to shoot up, Nilsen watched as Sinclair injected himself with heroin and fell into a stupor. He then strangled him with an improvised ligature made of a necktie and string, and then bathed him and laid him on the bed, reportedly whispering to the corpse: 'Nothing can hurt you now.'

Sinclair was not so comprehensively disposed of as the other Cranley Gardens victims. After the now standard routine of dissection, dismemberment and filleting, the majority of his remains were stored in plastic bags. The boiled head, upper torso and arms were put into the tea chest in his living room; the lower torso and legs into a cubby hole beneath his bathtub.

The reason? Complaints had been made about problems with blocked drains at 23 Cranley Gardens. Most astonishingly, one of those complaints had been made by Nilsen himself.

*

On 4 February 1983, Dennis Nilsen wrote a letter to the management agency in charge of his building: toilets were not flushing properly, and the blockage could not be cleared. The situation for the residents, he said, was intolerable.

A plumber was called, but could not fix the problem, and specialists from Dyno-Rod were brought in. When their investigator entered the drains through a manhole, what he saw horrified him. Thick sludge lined the floor of the sewer, a putrid trail leading back into the waste pipes from the house. It looked – and smelled – like animal flesh. As Nilsen and the other tenants watched, the sludge was removed, but with the evening drawing in and light fading, there was little more that could be done that day. Tomorrow, the man from Dyno-Rod said, he would return and investigate exactly what the flesh-like substance was.

That night, the lumps of meat disappeared. But the following day, when the investigators probed deeper, they found more: four bones and further scraps of flesh were discovered in a pipe that linked to the attic flat. They were taken to a mortuary, where it was confirmed they were human.

When Nilsen returned from work on 9 February, three policemen were waiting for him. They told him that following the discovery of human flesh in the drains, they would like to come into his flat to discuss matters further.

Calm and dispassionate as always, Nilsen let them in. The flat reeked. As the officers gagged from the stench, one exclaimed:

'Don't mess about, where's the rest of the body?'

Cold as ice, Dennis Nilsen pointed towards the wardrobe. He was taken into custody immediately.

Once at the police station, he added that they might want to also check the tea chest, as well as the cubby hole under his bath. Oh – and while they were about it, they may as well have a look around 195 Melrose Avenue where, he calmly stated, he had killed 'twelve or thirteen' men.

Nilsen was sentenced to life in prison on 4 November 1983. He was 38 years old, and would die behind bars 35 years later. While incarcerated he wrote a 400-page autobiography, graphically and matter-of-factly detailing his murders, without remorse, regret, or, it seemed, emotion. An extract from that journal might be the closest we will ever get to a 'why' behind the cold-blooded horror of his crimes:

'I could only relate to a dead image of the person I could love,' he wrote. 'It seems necessary for them to have been dead in order that I could express those feelings which were the feelings I held sacred for my grandfather . . . it was a pseudo-sexual, infantile love which had not yet developed and matured. The sight of them brought me a bitter sweetness and a temporary peace and fulfilment.'

FRED &

4

FRED & ROSE WEST

(UK, 1967–87, 12–30 VICTIMS)

When the dishevelled man first sat beside her at the bus stop, Rosemary Letts didn't pay him any mind. When he tried to make conversation, she gave him a good look up and down, but still remained unfazed. Although she had only just turned 15, Rosemary was well used to the attention of older men – and if the rumours around the Gloucestershire village where she lived were true, she actually courted their looks, their leers . . . and perhaps even more.

Older men hitting on her may have held a certain excitement for Rosemary, but this one looked like a tramp. She ignored him, and when he took the seat next to her on the bus and tried again to start a conversation, she stared out of the window.

The next day he did the same, and the day after. Gradually, she thawed. Despite his shabby clothes, his dirty stubble, his thick, messy hair, and his broad accent, he did possess an odd sort of charm. Although he was 13 years older than her (and, as she soon discovered, a father to two toddlers), he didn't talk to her like a child. Quite the reverse: if anything he was overly forward. Within a week she was not only responding in kind to his suggestive remarks, but had agreed to go on a date with him. By the end of the month the two were inseparable, and she quit her job in a bread shop to become nanny to his daughters.

Two years later she would kill one of those little girls, Charmaine, then aged just eight years old. Another nine bodies would follow, as well as at least two other murders committed by her besotted lover.

The 1969 chance encounter at the Cheltenham bus stop between Fred West and Rosemary Letts was an extraordinary coming together of two people apparently made for each other – joined by a twisted kind of love, but also by an unspeakable evil. Together, their story remains one of the saddest and most sordid episodes in British criminal history.

*

By the time he met Rosemary Letts in early 1969, Fred West was already a killer.

Born in 1941 into a family of farm labourers in the Herefordshire village of Much Marcle, Fred was the eldest of six children, and after leaving school at 15 worked as a farmhand. He also began to take an interest in the opposite sex – gaining a reputation at the local youth club dances as a pest and a groper, and on one occasion getting knocked two floors off the fire escape by an angry girl after he stuck his hand up her skirt.

In 1961 the groping took a more serious turn. In June of that year he was arrested on suspicion of child molestation after a 13-year-old from the village was discovered to be pregnant. When questioned, West appeared genuinely mystified: 'Doesn't everyone do it?' he asked the policemen. The case would collapse after the girl refused to give evidence.

The following year he married Rena Costello, a sometime prostitute and burglar, despite her being pregnant with another man's child, and moved to Scotland. Within months, baby Charmaine, who was mixed race, was born. A year later, the couple had a child together, whom they named Anna Marie.

Happy families it was not, however. Both Fred and Rena supplemented their income with petty crime and, in her case, prostitution – as well as embarking on numerous affairs and casual infidelities. The two babies were secondary, and were mostly looked after by 16-year-old Anne McFall, a troubled girl who had all but moved in with them. In 1965 Fred, Rena, Anne and the two children moved to Gloucestershire, and Fred took a job in an abattoir, where he became skilled at butchering carcasses.

He had also become increasingly violent. Both women were subjected to beatings and sexual assaults, while the children would often spend their days either ignored, or else confined to their beds. After Anne became pregnant with Fred's child, Rena fled back to Glasgow.

Whatever her failings as a mother, or weaknesses as a person, it seems Rena at least tried to look after her children. Without her, they were at the mercy of their father.

In July 1967, Anne McFall, then 18 years old and eight months pregnant, disappeared. Her remains would be found 27 years later buried at the edge of a cornfield close to their home. Her corpse had been dismembered, and several of her finger bones were missing. Her wrists showed signs of having been bound with the belt from a dressing gown. When questioned, Fred claimed that she had run away.

The following year, another girl disappeared. Mary Bastholm, a pretty 15-year-old who waitressed at a favourite café of Fred's, was abducted from a bus stop in Gloucester. Her body has never been found, but Fred West later told police he had killed her after raping her in his car. At around the same time, Gloucester was hit by a spate of sexual assaults on teenage girls – all of which remain unsolved.

If Rosemary Letts was concerned about the disappearance of Mary Bastholm, or the attacks on other girls in the area, she didn't show it. Shortly after her sixteenth birthday she moved full-time into Fred's Gloucester flat; before she was 17 she gave birth to their first child together: Heather.

Fred West's marriage to Rena Costello had been tempestuous; his relationship with Anne McFall one of coercion, control and abuse; but with Rose he found someone who was his equal – and whose sensibilities were every bit as narcissistic and depraved as his own. Whatever money Fred made was bolstered with the proceeds of low-level crime and petty theft; and before long Rose began working as a prostitute from their flat, with the two little girls and the baby left to their own devices in the room next door as she entertained her 'gentlemen friends'.

In December of 1970, Fred was sentenced to six and a half months in prison for the theft of car tyres and a tax disc, and, left alone with the three children, Rose's selfishness escalated into sadism. The two older girls were regularly beaten for no reason other than her entertainment – a favourite of Rose's was to strip them naked, bind and gag them, force them to stand on a chair and then thrash them with a large wooden spoon. Charmaine, with darker skin and no genetic connection to either Fred or Rose, invariably got the worst of it. Baby Heather was spared – for now.

In late June 1971, just days before Fred was released from prison, the violence turned fatal.

Only Rose knows for sure whether her murder of eight-year-old Charmaine West was the accidental result of a beating gone too far, or the inadvertent consequence of a spontaneous flash of anger, or even a planned and cold-blooded execution – and Rose is not telling. But in the days following her death, she calmly informed Charmaine's school, her sister and her few friends that Rena had returned from Scotland to take her daughter back. After Anna Marie asked why her mum had left her behind, she was told: 'She wouldn't want you. You're the wrong colour.'

The only person she did not lie to was Fred. When he came

home from prison, she told him the truth. Charmaine was in the coal cellar.

His reaction was horrifyingly practical. Having already buried two teenage girls, Fred now dug another grave, just outside their back door. Before he filled it in, he made sure to cut off the fingers and toes of the girl he had brought up since her birth – mementoes of an unhappy, and pathetically short, life.

In August she would be joined by her mother.

Rose's explanation that Charmaine had gone to live with Rena may have worked initially, but once Rena herself turned up, awkward questions would soon be asked. And barely two months after Charmaine's murder, Rena did just that, arriving at their Gloucester flat and demanding to know exactly where her daughter was.

Fred did the only thing he could think of: he killed her too. This time he did more than just remove the fingers and toes from the corpse – when Rena's body was discovered more than two decades later in a field close to the village of Much Marcle, it had been comprehensively dismembered, with the separate parts placed into plastic bags. With the remains was a length of metal tubing.

The following year Fred and Rose were married, and moved to a new house, in Cromwell Street, close to Gloucester city centre.

*

Between them, Fred and Rose West had killed four times in three years. Once settled at 25 Cromwell Street they would plumb new depths of evil – and add another eight young women to their body count.

In order to finance the purchase of the three-storey house, the upper two floors were converted into bedsits for lodgers, with the Wests – plus Anna Marie, Heather and their new baby, Mae – living on the ground floor, and with sole access to the garden.

One of the upstairs rooms was retained for Rose's professional use: soon after the birth of Mae, she placed a series of adverts in classified 'contact' magazines and resumed her career as a prostitute. Fred not only encouraged her in this, but enjoyed watching her through hidden peepholes, and even installed a baby monitor in the room so that he could listen to her entertain clients from elsewhere in the house. Over the following 11 years Rose would give birth to another six children; the true identity of their various fathers has never been established.

Rose wasn't averse to giving out freebies, either, and would regularly have sex with lodgers, friends and work colleagues of Fred's. Sometimes the couple would engage in threesomes with other women – sessions that became increasingly sadistic as Fred and Rose used bondage, violence and pain to get their kicks.

And still it wasn't enough.

In September 1972, they began abusing Anna Marie. The eight-year-old would be taken into the cellar, stripped and bound by Rose, before being raped by her father, while being mocked by her stepmother. By the age of 13, she was forced to join Rose as a prostitute, with her age being advertised as a 'barely legal' 16.

That same autumn, 17-year-old Caroline Owens, who the Wests had hired as a nanny, quit her job after less than two months after becoming increasingly uncomfortable about her employers' constant sexual innuendos – as well as the steady stream of men passing through the house to Rose's special upstairs room.

Fred and Rose followed her as she left – and persuaded her to let them give her a lift back to her mother's house. Once she got in the car, they beat her into unconsciousness, before returning to Cromwell Street. When Owens woke up, she was in the cellar, naked, her arms tied and duct tape over her mouth. For the rest of the night she was subjected to prolonged and brutal sexual abuse by the couple, with the assaults punctuated by floggings with a leather belt and smothering with a pillow. When they finally tired of her, they left her on the floor of the cellar, locked the door, and went to bed.

Caroline Owens woke the next morning to see her torturers standing above her again. This time, however, they wanted something different: now she had seen the error of her ways, they wondered, would she consider coming back to work for them again?

Despite her shock, her pain, her terror, Owens made the best decision of her life. 'Of course I would,' she said, and after offering to clean up the mess, promised to take the children's clothes to the launderette later that day.

She never made it to the launderette – but instead fled to the police. Fred and Rose West were charged with assault, indecent assault, actual bodily harm, and rape. Finally, it seemed, the horrors of 25 Cromwell Street would be stopped.

By the time the case was due to be tried, in January 1973, Owens, terrified of facing her tormentors and panicked about being cross-examined by their lawyer, told police she could not face testifying in person. Without her, the case collapsed: the assault and rape charges were dropped, and Fred and Rose were let off with a £50 fine.

Far from being stopped, the horrors of 25 Cromwell Street had barely begun. Three months after walking free from court, the couple committed their first known murder together. Fred West was 31 years old; Rose still just 19.

*

The debasement that had begun with Rose's teenage prostitution and led to the rape of their own daughter and torture of Caroline Owens would inevitably climax with murder. Fred and Rose had both killed before – but arguably each of those killings had stemmed from rage. Now, they looked to murder as the ultimate expression of their twisted desires.

In April 1973, 19-year-old Lynda Gough, who had previously had a relationship with one of the Wests' lodgers (and possibly with Rose herself) was lured into the cellar. There her mouth was sealed shut with surgical tape to stifle her screams, her wrists bound with knotted string and fabric, and she was strangled to death, most likely after hours of rape and torture. Afterwards,

Fred once more carefully dismembered her body, saved some of the smaller bones as keepsakes, and buried the remains beneath the garage. When her mother called to ask if Fred or Rose knew where her daughter was, they told her Lynda had been asked to leave the house after striking one of the children.

Unlike Gough, Fred and Rose West's next four victims would all be strangers to Cromwell Street; like Gough, they would all be young women subjected to horrific agonies before they were killed.

In November 1973, 15-year-old Carol Ann Cooper was abducted in Worcester after a night at the cinema. She too had her mouth bound with surgical tape, but once they were in the cellar, Fred suspended the teenager from wooden beams in the ceiling – where the couple kept her for days before finally tiring of her. A month later, 21-year-old Lucy Partington was also snatched from a bus stop: the university student was tortured for a week on Fred's home-made rack until her murder, mutilation and burial.

The following year another two bodies were added beneath the cellar floor: Therese Siegenthaler, a 21-year-old sociology student originally from Switzerland, was picked up as she hitchhiked in April 1974; in November, 15-year-old Shirley Hubbard was abducted from a bus stop as she travelled home from a date. When her remains were discovered, Hubbard's head had been completely wrapped in tape, with a small rubber tube inserted into her nostrils to allow her to breathe as she was tortured.

Five months later the Wests claimed a sixth victim together, and their tenth overall. Juanita Mott had been a former lodger at 25 Cromwell Street: she was picked up hitchhiking on 12 April 1975 before being drugged, gagged and smuggled into the cellar. The 18-year-old was trussed up and suspended from the ceiling with washing line before suffering the most brutal and sadistic torture of any of their victims to date, kept alive for hours in excruciating pain and barely able to move as she was repeatedly beaten and sexually abused before being strangled to death and dismembered.

Mott would be the last young woman to be buried in the cellar: after her murder, Fred concreted over the floor and converted the area into a bedroom for their eldest children. He and Rose would not kill again for three years.

The gap between the killings of Juanita Mott and their next victim, 18-year-old Shirley Robinson, has puzzled detectives and true-crime enthusiasts for decades. Did the extreme depravity of the torments they inflicted upon Mott scare even them into backing off? Did the loss of their dungeon mean they no longer had the dedicated space to kill in the manner they wanted to? Were they worried that police investigating the missing girls might join the dots with the assault and rape charges brought by former nanny Caroline Owens?

Whatever the answer, Fred and Rose West are not known to have killed again until the spring of 1978. The motive this time was not overtly sexual, but a return to the 'anger killings' that began their bloody campaign. Shirley Robinson was not only a former lodger at Cromwell Street, where she too worked as a prostitute, but had also participated in several of the Wests' threesomes. At the time of her murder she was eight months pregnant with Fred's child.

Although Rose was happy to share sexual partners with her husband, it seems she did not want anyone else having his children – and on 10 May 1978 Robinson disappeared. When her remains were discovered buried in the garden, the unborn baby had been cut out of her womb.

There would be one more sexually motivated murder, and one more anger killing – perhaps the most shocking of them all – before Fred and Rose West were finally brought to justice.

Sixteen-year-old Alison Chambers was a runaway whom the Wests had taken into Cromwell Street in the summer of 1979. Within weeks she too had been raped, tortured and killed: Fred later told his solicitor that her death was unplanned, but the result of Rose becoming 'too bloody vicious' with her. Her dismembered remains were also buried in the garden overflow cemetery.

And then . . . nothing for eight years.

If there's confusion about the Wests' previous murder hiatus, the period between 1979 and 1987 seems easier to explain. During this period not only was Rose pregnant much of the time – giving birth to a further three babies – but she and Fred had also directed their twisted impulses away from students and teenage runaways and onto their own children.

Anna Marie West had been the subject of Fred's sexual abuse since she was eight years old – by the time she was 15 she was not only being forced to work as a prostitute, but Fred and Rose would also loan her out to friends for their 'entertainment'. In

1979 she ran away after miscarrying, and Fred and Rose turned their attention to their younger daughters, Heather and Mae, then aged just nine and seven.

Through the early and mid-1980s both girls were regularly raped by their father, with Fred telling them: 'I made you; I can do what I like with you.' Heather, as the older child, came off the worst – by 1986, her school had expressed concern that she had become withdrawn and angry, as well as refusing to change clothes for PE lessons.

Nothing came of the school's concerns, but Fred and Rose became increasingly worried that Heather might have confided in one of her friends or teachers about the treatment she received at the hands of her parents. Once again, they took matters into their own hands, in the only way they knew how.

On 19 June 1987, Heather West was murdered by her own mother and father, dismembered with a kitchen knife, and became the final body buried in the backyard of 25 Cromwell Street. In a final sickening twist, Fred had her 14-year-old brother Stephen dig her grave, on the pretence of creating a fish pond for the garden. He and her other siblings were told she had run away.

*

The killing of their oldest daughter was the final act of Fred and Rose West's 20-year trail of murder, but it would not be the end of the horrors they inflicted at Cromwell Street. For a further five years they would continue to abuse their remaining children, even joking with them that the punishment for telling anyone about the assaults would be to 'end up under the patio like Heather'.

Finally, in 1992, youngest daughter Louise, then 13, told a school friend that her father had been raping her. Her friend told her mother; she went to the police. The house was searched, and after a huge cache of sexual paraphernalia and home-made pornography was discovered, all of the children were placed into care.

After Anna Marie came forward and gave a statement about the abuse she had received, Fred West was charged with three counts of rape and one of buggery, with Rose additionally charged with child cruelty. Anna Marie also suggested police should speak to Heather – if they could find her.

It took a further two years of dogged investigation until the truth was revealed. After failing to track down Heather West, detectives became increasingly convinced that she might be dead. On 23 February 1994, they obtained a search warrant, and began to dig up the garden at 25 Cromwell Street.

The next day Fred confessed to the murder; and over the following two weeks every one of the young women buried in his cellar and garden were recovered. The missing finger and toe bones removed as grisly mementoes have never been found.

On 30 June, Fred was charged with 12 counts of murder. Initially he claimed to have carried out all of the killings alone, but by the end of the year he changed his mind. Rose, he now said, not only knew of the murders, but was complicit in every one of them bar that of McFall. It was to be the last act of a vile life: on New Year's Day 1995, he hanged himself in his prison cell. His suicide note ended: 'In perfect peace he waits for Rose, his wife.'

On 22 November 1995, Rose West was found guilty of the murders of 10 girls and young women, including her own daughter Heather. She remains imprisoned in Yorkshire.

The wretched consequences of Fred and Rosemary West's 25 years together did not end with his death and her incarceration. The pain and suffering they caused continued to send shockwaves to those around them for years after. Before his suicide Fred confessed to a further 18 murders; the identity and whereabouts of those victims remain unknown to this day.

The Wests were also responsible for the deaths – and attempted suicides – of another six people, including three of their own children.

Caroline Owens, who had suffered abuse and torture in the Cromwell Street cellar before escaping, attempted suicide in 1973 after her rape and assault case against Fred and Rose collapsed. Fred's younger brother John and friend Terence Crick both killed themselves in 1996: at the time of his death John was on trial for the rape of Anna Marie West.

Anna Marie herself attempted suicide in 1995, two weeks after testifying at her stepmother's trial; in 1999 she tried again, jumping from a bridge into the River Severn. Three years afterwards, Fred and Rose's oldest son Stephen West tried to hang himself – and he was later jailed for nine months on seven counts of unlawful sex with a 14-year-old.

In 2020, after suffering from psychiatric issues and drug

addiction for years, youngest son Barry West died from a fatal drug overdose. He was 40 years old.

Rose West continues to maintain her innocence.

5

JOHN BUNTING, ROBERT WAGNER & JAMES VLASSAKIS

(AUSTRALIA, 1992–9, 12 VICTIMS)

When Clinton Tresize accepted an invitation to the home of John Bunting in August 1992, he had no reason to expect anything but the beginning of a closer relationship with his neighbour. Since moving into his house on Waterloo Corner Road in the Adelaide suburb of Salisbury North, 25-year-old Bunting and his wife Veronika Tripp had quickly grown close to several of their neighbours. Now the socially awkward Tresize, five years his junior, hoped to be among the charismatic Bunting's inner circle.

Chief among those friends were Robert Wagner, also 20, and his lover Vanessa Lane, a pre-op transexual nearly twice Wagner's age who was formerly known as Barry Lane. It was through Lane that Tresize came to be invited to Bunting's house that day. He was not asked to visit because Bunting wanted to become friends with him: he was asked because Lane had told Bunting that Clinton Tresize was a paedophile.

The young man had barely made it into the living room before Bunting smashed a shovel across his head. As he crumpled, Bunting struck him again and again, in the face, across the chest, the arms, the legs – the heavy metal slab of the shovel cracking bones, ripping skin, crushing internal organs.

Within minutes it was over. As the blood pooled, Wagner and Lane helped Bunting clear up the mess, before loading the body into his car and driving 20 miles north into the countryside, where they buried it in a shallow grave. The mood was light, and as they drove, Bunting jokingly referred to their victim as 'Happy Pants'.

Tresize's corpse would not be found for another two years, and Bunting would not be identified as his murderer for another five years after that. By then, Bunting's body count would be in double figures.

The murder of Clinton Tresize was the first in a bloody spree led by Bunting and assisted by Wagner and others. The murders have a particular bizarreness to them because in each one the killers and victims were well known to each other – in some cases actually related – and in two instances one of the murder gang even became a victim themselves. Four of the twelve victims were living with one or other of the killers at the time of their murders; many suffered unimaginable tortures before they were dispatched.

For seven years, predators and targets alike moved in the same Salisbury North circle: a complicated and incestuous clique made up of Adelaide's underclass, a socially isolated, culturally deprived and often exploited section of society that most Australians preferred not to see, and that accordingly kept to itself.

In such an environment, a man with charisma and intelligence could dominate.

The individual who would become known as Australia's worst serial killer did not murder for sexual pleasure, or for money, or even, for the most part, from anger. He killed because he could. He killed because killing made him feel powerful.

*

John Bunting was 25 years old when he moved to Salisbury North, and already a seriously damaged young man. As an eight-year-old he had been beaten and sexually abused by the older brother of one of his friends, and the lasting psychological effects of that abuse were to affect him in profound – and profoundly dangerous – ways.

While still a child he began to take pleasure in torturing animals – starting with insects, which he would burn with acid, before progressing onto bigger prey: as a young man he would trap pet cats and dogs, which he would then kill and skin.

The abuse affected him in other ways too. As he grew into adulthood, Bunting nursed the shame and anger he felt into a deep hatred of paedophiles or any one he felt to be 'degenerate'; by the time he came to be living in Waterloo Corner Road, he had constructed what he called a 'rock spider wall' (after the Australian slang term for a child molester) across the whole side of a spare room in the house. Modelled on criminal investigation boards used by detectives to link evidence with suspects, this was an elaborate display of paper notes joined by lines of pink and blue wool to create an interconnected web of people he suspected to be paedophiles, homosexuals and drug users. In the middle of the wall was a single word: 'GUILTY'.

Bunting would spend hours with his rock spider wall, amassing information about his suspects before making contact: initially he contented himself with simply trying to scare them, telephoning them to warn they would 'get what's coming'. Later he would take more decisive action.

Bunting's nascent psychopathic tendencies were also reflected in his choice of jobs. After leaving school without qualifications he first worked in a crematorium, where he was considered a diligent and dedicated employee, and then at the South Australian Meat Corporation, where he not only learned how to slaughter animals, but told his friends that he took huge pleasure in doing so.

Despite all this, Bunting was nevertheless a charismatic and magnetic personality, and surrounded himself with people whose own psychological damage made them naturally subservient to him. Wife Veronika Tripp was later described in court as suffering from physical and mental disabilities, and 'a person of limited capacity'; his later partners in crime were also in thrall to the man they felt operated in a realm above the normal rules of morality.

It was all to foster Bunting's god complex – like a cult leader, the more crazed he got and the more his power grew, the more those around him were magnetized. As well as Robert Wagner and Barry Lane, he was to draw another five men and women into his murderous orbit.

If the murder of Clinton 'Happy Pants' Tresize was to be the first time Bunting took his simmering hatred of suspected paedophiles to fatal lengths, it did not mark the beginning of his real killing spree: he would not commit another murder for three years, and then would wait for a further twenty months before striking again.

When Tresize's remains were discovered in the remote township of Lower Light in August 1994, how and why he had ended up there remained a mystery to police. And back in the suburbs of North Adelaide, his killer had moved on from Veronika Tripp to another woman, Elizabeth Harvey. She too was wholly under his spell – as was one of her sons, 14-year-old James Vlassakis, a withdrawn boy who was also a heroin addict and on a methadone programme.

A short time later, perhaps emboldened by the lack of any leads in the Clinton Tresize case, Bunting murdered for a second time.

Once again, the target was someone from his rock spider wall. Once again, he did not act alone. And as would now be the pattern for all the subsequent murders, once again, killer and victim were closely connected.

Ray Davies was a 26-year-old intellectually disabled man who lived in a caravan behind the home of his ex-girlfriend Suzanne Allen – a woman 20 years older who had previously also had a relationship with Bunting. In December 1995, Allen told Bunting that two of her grandsons had claimed Davies had made sexual advances towards them. It was an effective death sentence.

On Christmas Day, Bunting, Wagner and Elizabeth Harvey entered Davies' caravan. Harvey held a knife, Wagner carried jumper cables. Before the confused man could react, Harvey stabbed him in the leg, and as he doubled over in agony, Wagner looped the cables around his neck and pulled tight. He lost consciousness within seconds.

This time, however, there was to be no quick death. As far as Bunting was concerned, simply killing a rock spider was too easy a punishment for their crimes – he wanted the paedophile to suffer before they died. Unconscious, bleeding, but still alive, Davies was loaded by the two men into the boot of Bunting's car, who drove him 90 minutes east, deep into the desert and an abandoned house in the tiny village of Bakara.

Ray Davies woke up naked in a bathtub to find Bunting and Wagner standing over him. Bunting held a heavy metal pole. If being stabbed and strangled had been agonizing, it was nothing compared to the horrors of his final minutes of life. Swinging the pole like a baseball bat, Bunting smashed it over and over again at the helpless man – targeting his genitals, and his genitals only. He kept swinging until Davies was dead.

This time they did not leave the body in the desert, but instead hauled what was left of him back into the car and returned to Salisbury North, before burying him in the backyard of Bunting's Waterloo Corner Road house.

As with Clinton Tresize, the disappearance of Ray Davies went completely unnoticed by the authorities. The North Adelaide society of misfits and dropouts was effectively off the radar, fallen through the gaps of civilized society – so much so that Bunting even continued to collect Davies' social security benefits years later.

*

If the relationship between Bunting and Davies was complicated, his next victim would be an even more convoluted combination of Bunting's incestuous Salisbury North circle.

In the months following the second killing, Wagner and Barry Lane ended their relationship, both taking new partners – in Wagner's case, moving in with a woman named Veronica Mills, a single mother with whom he later had a son.

Through Mills, Bunting met Michelle – formerly Michael – Gardiner, a 19-year-old transgender woman who lived in a room in the same residence as Mills's cousin, Nicole Zuritta. Despite Wagner's own bisexuality, he instantly took against Gardiner, whose exaggeratedly camp behaviour he found intimidating.

The final straw came one afternoon in the summer of 1997: Wagner chanced upon Gardiner playing with Mills's children – as he watched, he saw Gardiner place her hand over the child's mouth. Infuriated at what he believed to be a sign of potential abuse, he went straight to Bunting.

They had already dealt with two 'degenerates'. Now it was Michelle Gardiner's turn.

Bunting's first victim had been beaten to death with a shovel; his second stabbed, strangled and ultimately mutilated with an iron pole. For Gardiner he changed tactic again. The 19-year-old was bundled into a shed, where a makeshift noose was constructed. While one man held her down, the other tightened the noose until she collapsed; every time Gardiner's legs gave way they hauled her back up again, slapped her back into consciousness, and repeated the process. After her heart finally gave out, they stuffed her corpse into a barrel. In order to get the lid on securely, they had to saw off her left foot.

Bunting and his collaborators had killed three times in three years with apparent impunity. Now they changed up a gear. Before the end of 1997 they would slaughter another three times – and the next victim was one of their own.

After Wagner and Vanessa Lane had split, she too had formed new relationships, taking an 18-year-old lover by the name of Thomas Trevilyan, as well as getting engaged to a woman and moving into her house in the nearby suburb of Hectorville.

Lane had become increasingly worried about her part in the killing of Clinton Tresize: in October, word reached Bunting that Lane had been telling friends about the murder; and he also heard that Lane's relationship with Trevilyan had begun when the boy was still under the age of consent.

Bunting had never liked the older transgender woman, tolerating Lane only because of her relationship with Wagner, and – more importantly – because she was a good source of information on the activities of suspected paedophiles in the area. Now, with Lane and Wagner no longer together, Lane apparently shooting her mouth off about Clinton Tresize, and, most crucially, the revelation that she was a paedophile herself, there was nothing to hold him back.

On 17 October, accompanied by Wagner and Thomas Trevilyan, Bunting confronted Lane. First he forced her to call her mother: with Trevilyan providing the script, Lane explained that not only was she moving to Queensland, but she no longer wanted anything to do with her. Once they had hung up on the distraught woman, the real business began.

Ray Davies and Michelle Gardiner had both suffered agonies before dying; now Bunting took the abuse to another level entirely. For hours Vanessa Lane was meticulously and mercilessly tortured, Bunting producing a pair of pliers and carefully using them to crush each one of her toes in turn. Her screams were stifled by strangulation. After she finally died, her body was dismembered and stuffed into another barrel to be stored in Bunting's shed.

Although – just as he had done with Ray Davies – Bunting assumed control of Lane's subsequent welfare payments, the money was never a motive for murder. The posthumous government cheques were nothing more than a bonus: the real reward lay in the removal of another rock spider, in the further assertion of Bunting's superiority, and in his subsequent increased hold over his gang.

The following month Suzanne Allen disappeared. The ex-girlfriend of Bunting who had provided him with an apparent justification for killing Ray Davies would later be discovered buried in the backyard of Bunting's Waterloo Corner Road property, her remains wrapped in 11 plastic bags. When later questioned, he would claim that she died of a heart attack.

At the same time Bunting also began to grow concerned about Thomas Trevilyan. The 18-year-old had a history of paranoid behaviour and hallucinations: by 4 November, barely three weeks after he had helped kill his former lover, he was acting increasingly erratically. After the boy attacked Wagner's girlfriend's son's puppy with a knife, Bunting decided he had become a liability. He and Wagner drove him to the woods outside Adelaide and hanged him from a tree. In a small act of mercy, Trevilyan was at least spared torture; when his body was found the next day, the coroner ruled his death suicide.

*

Bunting and Wagner had killed six times, with two of their victims being erstwhile accomplices in their crimes. Now they would draw another acolyte into their circle.

After Bunting had moved in with Elizabeth Harvey, her son James Vlassakis had grown to idolize his new father figure. By early 1998 he was just turned 18, and had been addicted to heroin and methadone since his early teens.

Although Bunting was fond of his effective stepson, he was not so enamoured of the company he kept: Vlassakis's addictions meant he moved in North Adelaide's most socially deprived circles, a shifting community of junkies and dropouts, many of whom lived on the streets.

One of these was Gavin Porter, a 29-year-old heroin addict and schizophrenic who alternated between sleeping rough and stints in mental institutions. He was a regular visitor to the house Vlassakis shared with Bunting and his mother – even, despite Bunting's objections, staying for days or weeks on end, sleeping on the sofa or in his car parked in their driveway.

For months, Bunting tolerated his presence: finally, in April 1998, he snapped. After pricking himself on a syringe that Porter had left discarded in his living room, he declared his unwelcome guest to be another dangerous degenerate: as Porter slept that night, he and Wagner jumped him and strangled him to death.

Bunting barely even considered his seventh killing a murder at all, and before he stuffed the corpse into yet another barrel, he summoned Vlassakis to bear witness to the dead body. Porter was a 'waste', he was told, and should serve as a warning to all those who no longer deserved to live.

James Vlassakis took the words to heart. In August that year he provided Bunting with his next victim – half-brother Troy Youde, whom he claimed had sexually abused him when he was just 13 and Troy 16. Now, he told Bunting and Wagner, he wanted to join his heroic surrogate father in ridding the world of another degenerate.

Youde was surprised in his bed as he slept, and handcuffed while the three men beat him near-senseless. He was then dragged to the bath, where the beatings continued – though this time, Bunting introduced a new angle to the torture. Once again producing his pliers, he told Youde that after every blow he was to address his attackers as 'Sir', 'God', or 'Master': inability to do so to Bunting's satisfaction would see a toe snapped.

By the time he was strangled and placed in a barrel, Youde's feet were little more than a pulp of bloody flesh and splintered bone.

Over the following three months, Bunting and Wagner – assisted by Vlassakis – would kill a further three times. In September 1998 Fred Brooks, an 18-year-old air cadet who Bunting was convinced was abusing young girls, was tortured to death after being lured by Vlassakis to a non-existent party; in October, 19-year-old Gary O'Dwyer, a neighbour of Bunting's who was physically and mentally disabled, was similarly tortured and killed in the home of Bunting's friend Mark Haydon – his crime seemed to be little more than that Bunting considered him 'weak' and a burden on society. A month later, Haydon's own wife Elizabeth was killed after Bunting began to suspect she had learned of O'Dwyer's murder. Far from being distraught, horrified or even angry that Bunting had murdered his wife, Haydon is reported to have laughed when he was shown her dead body.

By the time of her murder the issue of where to store all the barrels in which the killers had been hiding the bodies had become pressing. The problem was apparently solved by Mark Haydon, who suggested renting an abandoned bank vault in the rural community of Snowtown, around 100 miles north of Adelaide.

One by one the barrels were driven to Snowtown, unloaded, and rolled into the vault. Bunting also decided the remote spot would be the perfect location for future murders – the lack of potential witnesses and the thick walls of the vault meant they could torture their victims for hours without fear of attracting attention.

In May the following year, the serial killers struck for the final time. Once again, their victim was another of Vlassakis's siblings, this time his stepbrother David Johnson. Johnson's crime was not that he had abused Vlassakis, but simply that he was overly fastidious about his personal appearance. Bunting decided that was evidence enough that he was homosexual, and by extension a likely paedophile. Vlassakis tricked him into accompanying him to buy a second-hand computer – leading him to Snowtown, where Bunting and Wagner were waiting. After they had finished with him, the murderers sliced off a piece of Johnson's flesh, fried it, and ate it.

David Johnson would be the last victim of John Bunting's brutal wave of self-righteous murder.

If Snowtown had been chosen because of its tiny population and remote location, those factors would ultimately be the killers' downfall. What few people did live in Snowtown could not fail to notice the sudden activity around the old bank – and when police investigating the disappearance of Elizabeth Haydon began to look into the associates of her husband, the trail soon led to John Bunting.

Bunting, Wagner and Haydon were arrested on 21 May 1999, and James Vlassakis five days after that. As the full horror of the seven-year murder campaign began to unfold, with further corpses dug up in Bunting's old home, the trial grew into the longest and most expensive in the history of South Australia. Bunting was eventually convicted of 11 murders, Wagner of 10. Vlassakis was convicted of four, and the final conspirator, Mark Haydon, received a sentence of 25 years for his role in helping dispose of the bodies.

None of the gang were ever convicted of the murder of Suzanne Allen. Charges against Bunting were eventually dropped after a hung jury decided there was not enough evidence to convict.

From the first murder of Clinton Tresize in 1992 to the final killing of David Johnson seven years later, Bunting, Wagner and their accomplices, acolytes, enablers and ardent hangers-on had accounted for 12 victims, many of them tortured and mutilated before they were killed. Like the leader of a religious cult, Bunting had exploited the social outcasts of North Adelaide's underclass, the damaged, addicted and abused, and either drawn them under his spell, or else inflicted a self-justified, terrible retribution upon them for their crimes, real and imaginary.

And like a religious cult member, his most devoted follower

maintained that twisted justification for murder even as he was jailed. At his sentencing, Robert Wagner asked to make a statement to the court.

'Paedophiles were doing terrible things to children,' he said. 'The authorities didn't do anything about it. I decided to take action. I took that action.'

6

IAN BRADY &
MYRA HINDLEY

(UK, 1963–5, 5 VICTIMS)

On paper, Ian Brady and Myra Hindley were not Britain's worst serial killers. On paper, they're not even close. But for anyone born in the second half of the twentieth century, the so-called Moors Murderers hold a horror unique in the country's cultural identity. Only ever convicted of three murders – though known to have killed two other children – they have nevertheless become national monsters, a personification of evil unmatched in modern British history.

Even the atrocities committed by Fred and Rosemary West – who murdered more than twice as many as Brady and Hindley

– pall before their crimes. Sometimes statistics don't tell the whole story.

The Moors Murders continue to resonate 60 years after they were carried out – not because of the number of victims, but because of who were killed, and the offhand manner of their executions and subsequent disposal of the bodies. Theirs was a slaughter of the innocents: casual, deliberate, emotionless, motiveless and unfathomably cruel.

*

When Myra Hindley met Ian Brady she was just 18 years old and widely regarded as a sensible, well-adjusted, popular young lady. Brought up in Gorton, a working-class suburb of east Manchester, she babysat for numerous families in the neighbourhood as a young teenager and became engaged on her seventeenth birthday to a local boy who held down a steady job at the local Co-op.

The engagement was short-lived. Sensible and well adjusted she may have seemed on the outside, but behind the smiles, Hindley was deeply discontented. When she was 15, a close friend had drowned while swimming in a reservoir – the experience instilled in her a deep sense of the fragility of life, and that there had to be more than the terraced streets and dead-end jobs that Gorton could offer.

As she approached her twenties Hindley was not about to settle for the life she seemed destined for: marriage, kids, and seemingly interminable years of struggling to make ends meet with only the local pub to provide any kind of distraction or excitement. She wanted more.

In January 1961 she found it.

Ian Brady had moved to Manchester with his mother from Glasgow in 1955 when he was 17. Although he was an intelligent child, his youth was marked by a series of run-ins with the police; Brady appeared before juvenile courts for a range of offences including housebreaking and burglary. After his move to Manchester the trouble continued: caught stealing lead, he was sentenced to two years in borstal, serving part of his sentence in Manchester's notorious Strangeways prison.

During his time behind bars, Brady became a voracious reader – and his literary tastes ran to the extremes. The works of the Marquis de Sade and Nietzsche were favourites, as well as Dostoyevsky's *Crime and Punishment*, and Hitler's *Mein Kampf*. He also taught himself bookkeeping, and after his release in 1959, took a job as a stock clerk with Millwards, a wholesale chemical distribution company in Gorton. Two years later, days after his twenty-third birthday, a new secretary joined the firm.

Myra Hindley was obsessed with the brooding, book-smart Brady almost from the moment she saw him. Her diary reveals a growing infatuation with the 'enigmatic, worldly' clerk, who always seemed to be reading battered, exotic-looking paperbacks by obscure foreign authors.

Nevertheless, for nearly a year he steadfastly ignored Hindley – his sullen disinterest only serving to increase his attraction to the lovestruck teenager – until finally, at the staff Christmas party, he asked her out on a date. Hindley's diary records a trip to the cinema to see the religious epic *King of Kings*; Brady remembered it as *Judgment at Nuremberg*, a dramatization of the Nazi military tribunals of 1947.

It was to be the beginning of a crash course in fascist ideology and Brady's twisted, narcissistic philosophy. Under his direction she began reading books about the Holocaust and other Nazi atrocities, as well as the writings of Nietzsche, Dostoyevsky, de Sade, and numerous accounts of torture, crime and pornography.

For the impressionable Hindley, Brady was the passport to the new, exciting world she had been craving. She withdrew from her other friends to spend all her free time with him, and even changed her appearance to appeal to his ideas of Aryan perfection, bleaching her hair blonde and wearing high boots, leather jackets and miniskirts. The couple spent days together in the library and the cinema, and their nights drinking German wine and taking pornographic photos of one another.

They also took regular trips out to Saddleworth Moor, a barren plateau of peat and bogland stretching from the eastern edge of Greater Manchester across the Pennines. In this desolate, windblown landscape the couple would walk for hours without seeing another soul, discussing Brady's ideas of transcending the stifling rules of conventional morality and breaking free from the dreary confines of working-class suburban Manchester.

Reading and talking about it was one thing: Brady insisted that if they were to have the courage of their convictions they had to demonstrate this shared new outlook in practical terms. The only question was how.

In July 1963, Brady told his girlfriend of his idea for the ultimate expression of their status as Nietzschean '*übermenschen*', operating in a realm beyond good and evil. 'Rape is not a crime,' he told her, 'it is a state of mind. Murder is a hobby and supreme pleasure.' Killing would be how they would express their supremacy. And killing an innocent would be the definitive existential act.

On 12 July 1963, Myra Hindley hired a van, and as evening drew in, drove off at a slow pace through the streets of Gorton. Behind her was Brady on a motorbike. He scanned the pavements as he rode, looking for a target.

At 7.30pm he found one. Eight-year-old Marie Ruck was walking home alone, skipping along the street towards them – as she approached, Brady flashed his headlight, signalling Hindley to stop.

She kept driving. When a furious Brady pulled alongside and demanded to know why she had ignored his instruction, she explained she recognized the girl as a neighbour of her mother and she knew that her disappearance would be big news in the tight-knit local community. They needed to find someone older.

Half an hour later, Brady once again flashed his headlight.

Walking away from them along a back street off Gorton Lane was a pretty 16-year-old in her best pale-blue coat and white high heels; as Hindley drew closer to the girl she realized that, once again, she knew her, this time as Pauline Reade, a friend of her younger sister.

If having a personal connection to their first potential victim gave Myra Hindley second thoughts, she didn't show it. Quite the reverse: she instead exploited that familiarity to pull over and say hello.

When Reade explained that she was on her way to a dance, Hindley was quick to offer her a lift, but asked if she minded taking a slight detour to Saddleworth Moor, about half an hour's drive away, to help her search for an expensive glove she had lost earlier that day. Reade, with no reason to distrust the sister of her friend, replied that she'd be happy to.

Brady followed the pair, and when they pulled off the road and into a layby, Hindley explained that he was her boyfriend, come to help with the search. As dusk fell, depending on whether you believe Hindley or Brady's account, either he and Reade set off over the deserted moor while Hindley stayed in the van, or else all three of them left together.

Pauline Reade would not return from Saddleworth Moor alive. In a spot just out of sight of the road near the landmark of Hollin Brown Knoll, she was violently raped, before having her throat cut with such force that she was nearly decapitated. The collar of her best blue coat was pushed into the four-inch gash in her voice box to soak up the blood.

The couple buried her where she lay and after loading Brady's motorbike into the back of the van, drove home to Manchester. As they neared Gorton, they passed Reade's mother, who, after being told by Pauline's friends that she had never shown up at the dance, was out looking for her missing daughter.

*

Four months later, the killers struck for a second time. The police had found no trace of the missing 16-year-old, and had drawn a blank on any leads as to where she might have gone. Emboldened by what Brady was describing as 'the perfect murder', on 23 November he and Hindley once again took to the streets of Manchester in search of another victim.

This time, perhaps mindful of the search that had followed Pauline Reade's disappearance, they left Gorton and headed five miles north-east in a hired Ford Anglia car, to Ashton-under-Lyne, on the eastern edge of the city – and also on the main route to Saddleworth Moor.

Rather than cruise the streets, Hindley parked up by the market, and after spotting 12-year-old John Kilbride standing alone, asked him to help her carry some boxes. The boy had gone to the market to earn some extra pocket money helping the stallholders pack up at the end of the day – he gladly assisted the glamorous-looking lady in exchange for a promised lift home.

Once in the car, she introduced Kilbride to Brady, who was sitting in the back seat, and he again explained that they were going to take a short detour to the moor to search for Hindley's lost glove.

John Kilbride was taken to the same lonely spot where the couple had killed Pauline Reade – and while Hindley waited in the van, Brady repeated the gruesome ritual, sexually assaulting the terrified boy before trying to slit his throat with a six-inch serrated blade. This time, however, the blade was too blunt; after repeated attempts to cut deep enough, Brady was forced to improvise. Untying his shoelace, he wrapped it around Kilbride's neck and pulled tight. The boy died in agony, and joined Pauline Reade under the Saddleworth sod.

If the disappearance of Pauline Reade was a mystery, the vanishing of John Kilbride sparked a huge manhunt. More than 500 posters were printed appealing for information and thousands of volunteers joined the police in searching the area around Ashton-under-Lyne; but as with Reade, they turned up no clues. Nobody had seen him talking to the lady with the peroxide blonde hair at the market, nobody had seen him getting into her car, nobody had seen them drive east into the moors.

Another seven months passed before they killed their third child – and once again, the couple stuck to their tried-and-tested modus operandi.

Keith Bennett, a cherub-faced 12-year-old with an infectious smile, was on his way to his grandmother's house in Longsight, near Gorton, on 16 June 1964. His mother had watched him safely over the Stockport Road, before leaving him to walk the last mile on his own.

He was barely out of her sight before Hindley stopped him. Would he mind helping her load some boxes into the back of her Mini Pickup van in exchange for a lift to his grandma's house? Although he had been warned about the dangers of accepting lifts from strange men, Bennett had no reason to fear a smiling, apparently helpless young woman – and climbed into the car without a second thought, unaware that Brady was lurking in the back.

He too was taken to the moor, and strangled with a piece of string. This time, the couple buried him in a different spot to their first two victims, and Brady later claimed that Hindley helped kill the boy, saying: 'I couldn't keep her away – she enjoyed it.'

Over the following months the killers would return to the shallow graves on the moors to pose for a series of photographs marking the spots where their victims lay. In one, Hindley poses in a leather coat, smiling bashfully; in another picture she plays with her dog while crouching over the grave of John Kilbride.

*

The Moors Murderers' fourth victim was to be their youngest, and her death by far the most shocking. With this killing the couple reached a level of cruelty that outstripped even their previous murders, and remains almost incomprehensible six decades later.

By late 1964 Hindley and Brady had moved from Gorton seven miles east, to a two-up, two-down house in Wardle Brook Avenue, Hyde. On 26 December, they drove to visit the Christmas funfair at Ancoats, just north of the city centre.

Also at the funfair was 10-year-old Lesley Ann Downey. The tiny, frail-looking child lived in a flat nearby with her mother and three brothers, and had gone to the fair with four other friends, on strict instructions she was to be home before it got dark.

At 5.30pm, the children began the short walk home – all except Lesley Ann, who paused by the dodgems, savouring one last look at the bright colours and rock 'n' roll music that lit up the darkening Mancunian dusk.

When her friends turned around to see where she was, she had already gone. As Lesley Ann gazed at the dodgem lights, Hindley had pounced, dropping her bags of shopping and asking the little girl's help in taking them to her car.

After that she didn't stand a chance. Bundled into the back seat by the waiting Brady, Downey was driven away within minutes. Unlike the others, however, she was not taken to the moors; this time the killers wanted to have some fun before killing her.

At Wardle Brook Avenue, the girl was taken upstairs, into a room that had been specially prepared for her. Brady's camera equipment was set up, as well as an audio tape recorder. Downey was bound, gagged with a scarf, and stripped naked, before being forced to pose for a series of pornographic photos. She was then repeatedly raped – her desperate screams for her mother and pleas to be allowed to go home ignored or laughed at as her tormentors only increased their torture and abuse.

Eventually her tiny body finally gave out – strangled to death either with a length of silk by Hindley as Brady held her down, or else garrotted by Brady with a piece of string while Hindley was out of the room, depending on which of the murderers you believe. Brady later claimed that, for weeks afterwards, Hindley would play in pubs with the cord she used to kill the girl, revelling in the open display of her depravity. The couple then left the little girl where she lay, retiring downstairs to watch television until they fell asleep.

The next morning they picked up Downey's body and what remained of her clothes, threw them in the boot of the car and drove to Saddleworth Moor. This time they returned to their favourite layby near Hollin Brown Knoll, and as Hindley stayed in the car, Brady set off across the scrub with a shovel. Lesley Ann Downey was buried naked, with her legs doubled up to her abdomen and her clothes arranged by her feet. Hindley remarked later that it was at that moment she decided: 'Now I know there's no God.'

*

Myra Hindley and Ian Brady had killed four times with absolute impunity, snatching their victims from the streets of Manchester, torturing, butchering and burying them – and leaving the police and their distraught families clueless as to what had become of the children.

Hindley was crucial to the couple's success. The ease with which she had convinced all four of their victims to enter her car meant that the most difficult part of their murder plans effectively became the easiest. Children were instinctively trusting of a woman. Nobody believed a woman would be capable of the kinds of crimes Myra Hindley would help commit.

If the murder of Lesley Ann Downey had convinced Hindley that there was no God, then it also cemented in Brady's mind the belief that he was above the conventional rules of society.

It felt like a vindication of his twisted Nietzschean philosophy: murder really had become 'a hobby and a supreme pleasure'.

His belief in his own invincibility was to be his downfall.

In the months following the killing of Keith Bennett, Brady had started grooming a person he hoped would become the third member of his cabal. Seventeen-year-old David Smith had married Hindley's sister Maureen in August 1964 (coincidentally, he was also a former boyfriend of the killers' first victim Pauline Reade) and, like Hindley herself, he had become fascinated by the intense, literate Brady from the moment he met him. As he had done with Hindley three years before, the older man gave Smith books to read, discussed philosophy and fascism with him, and laid out plans to rob a bank.

The teenager – who was no stranger to lawbreaking, thanks to convictions for actual bodily harm and housebreaking – was entranced. In the autumn of 1965, Brady decided it was time for Smith to undergo his full initiation.

On 6 October, Hindley and Brady drove into Manchester, and, in a break from their usual routine, she stayed in the car while he entered Manchester Central train station in search of a victim. Before long he reappeared with Edward Evans, a 17-year-old who he had picked up on the promise of alcohol and, according to Brady, sex.

Back at Wardle Brook Avenue, Brady opened a bottle of wine, and sent Hindley to fetch David Smith. When he arrived he was told to wait in the kitchen. What happened next can be told in Smith's own words, as he later related to the police:

'I waited about a minute or two then suddenly I heard a hell of a scream; it sounded like a woman, really high-pitched. Then the screams carried on, one after another really loud. Then I heard Myra shout, "Dave, help him," very loud. When I ran in I just stood inside the living room and I saw a young lad. He was lying with his head and shoulders on the couch and his legs were on the floor. He was facing upwards. Ian was standing over him, facing him, with his legs on either side of the young lad's legs. The lad was still screaming... Ian had a hatchet in his hand... he was holding it above his head and he hit the lad on the left side of his head with the hatchet. I heard the blow, it was a terrible blow, it sounded horrible.'

Smith might have been in awe of Brady's talk of Nietzsche and de Sade and the purity of an absolute existential act, but the bloody reality of watching him slaughter someone with an axe was something else entirely. Nevertheless, and despite his terror, he had enough wits about him to join in the couple's laughter, and help tidy up the blood and gore and stash the body in the spare bedroom. He left at 3am, promising to return later that morning to help bury the body on the moor.

David Smith did not return, but instead, after confessing to his wife what he had seen Brady and her sister do, called the police.

Within hours, Superintendent Bob Talbot knocked on Hindley's Wardle Brook Avenue door. After Evans's body was discovered in the spare room, Ian Brady was arrested on suspicion of murder.

*

Myra Hindley was not arrested with Brady, who initially claimed that Evans's death was an accident and that Hindley had 'only done what she had been told' – but after Smith told police that the couple had boasted to him about other murders, and that they had kept evidence of the killings in a left-luggage office at Manchester Central station, she was brought in and a thorough search carried out.

On 15 October two suitcases belonging to the couple were found. Inside was a grisly trove of murder mementoes, including nine photographs of a naked and terrified Lesley Ann Downey with a scarf tied around her mouth, as well as a 16-minute audio recording of the little girl screaming, crying, and begging to be allowed to go home to her mother, with Brady and Hindley's voices both audible in the background.

There were also numerous photographs of Saddleworth Moor, and the following day, using them to pinpoint possible grave locations, police discovered Downey's remains; five days after that, they recovered the badly decomposed corpse of John Kilbride. On 6 December, Ian Brady was charged with the murders of Downey, Kilbride and Evans, and Myra Hindley with those of Downey and Evans, and of harbouring Brady in the knowledge that he had killed John Kilbride.

Both denied all knowledge of the disappearance of Pauline Reade and Keith Bennett, and with their remains still undiscovered, murder charges could not be brought in those cases – though police were certain that the couple were responsible for their killings.

On 6 May 1966, after deliberating for just two hours, a jury found Hindley and Brady guilty on all counts. They would spend the rest of their lives in prison.

It would take until 1987 before Hindley and Brady would admit to killing Reade and Bennett, and after visits by both killers to the moors – under a massive police security operation – on 1 July 1987, 24 years after she was abducted, raped and had her throat slashed so viciously it nearly removed her head, Reade's remains were finally recovered, buried three feet below the surface of the moor, and just 100 yards from Lesley Ann Downey's grave.

'Myra Hindley and I . . . were a unified force, not two conflicting entities,' Brady later wrote. 'Existential philosophy melded with the spirituality of death and became predominant. We experimented with the concept of total possibility. Instead of the requisite Lady Macbeth, I got Messalina.'

Myra Hindley died in 2002, aged 60, after spending more than half her life in prison; she was followed by Ian Brady in 2017, aged 79.

Keith Bennett's body has never been found. The cherubic 12-year-old who was just trying to help a lady on his way to his grandma's house remains lost, somewhere on the windblown, desolate expanse of Saddleworth Moor. Alone, but not forgotten.

PART TWO

CARNAL OBSESSIONS

7

LARRY EYLER

(USA, 1982–4, 21+ VICTIMS)

Terre Haute, Indiana, is a small, quiet city of about 50,000 people just off Interstate 70, linking Indianapolis and St Louis. Despite its status as a major east–west arterial route covering over 2,000 miles from Utah to Maryland, the section of I-70 that passes through Indiana and neighbouring state Illinois is mostly deserted, a long, straight, windblown road through seemingly endless fields of corn and soybeans, the only relief from the tedious landscape being conurbations like Terre Haute.

On 3 August 1978, the residents of a house on the edge of Terre Haute were surprised by a frantic hammering at their door. When they answered, their surprise turned to horror: in front of them, barely upright on their porch, was a naked man, covered in blood. His hands were cuffed, and a knife was stuck in his chest. Before he passed out he begged for help.

Paramedics arrived within minutes, shortly followed by a sheriff's deputy. Although they were able to stabilize the young man, his injuries were so severe that he was unable to describe what had happened to him.

And then came something completely unexpected. Even as the sheriff's deputy puzzled over the attack, there was another knock at the door. The visitor identified himself as Larry Eyler, a 25-year-old house painter local to the area, and explained that he was responsible for the stabbing. He had picked the man up hitchhiking, they had got into an argument, and he had stabbed him accidentally. He also produced the key to unlock the handcuffs.

Eyler was arrested on the spot and after a search of his car turned up weapons, including a butcher's knife, a metal-tipped whip, tear gas and a sword, he was charged with aggravated battery and taken into custody.

Within a month he would be free again: even as the man he attacked recovered in hospital, Eyler's lawyers offered him $2,500 to drop all charges. He took the money.

Larry Eyler would go on to kill at least 21 other young men. Each of his victims would be picked up, apparently for sex, before being restrained, beaten and then stabbed in what one coroner would describe as 'tremendous rage', their bodies mutilated and dumped in fields or waste ground by the lonely highways of Indiana and Illinois. It would take years before police determined the growing number of corpses to be the work of one man.

*

Sex was the reason Larry Eyler killed – not for the fulfilment of desire, but rather for the opposite. When Eyler slashed and stabbed and gouged the men he picked up, it was the manifestation of his apparent hatred of sex – and of his own sexuality.

He was a person defined by self-loathing, a gay man who hated gay men, a sadomasochist for whom the sexual act was defined by pain and humiliation, and a murderer whose killings appeared to be the ultimate sadistic sexual act but often involved no sex at all.

Born in December 1952 into a working-class family in Indiana, Eyler endured a turbulent childhood. The youngest of four children, his parents divorced before he was three; his mother would remarry another three times, often to abusive, alcoholic men, and he spent extended periods in the care of foster families as she struggled to make ends meet.

The sense of loneliness and isolation that this gave the child was amplified further in adolescence as he struggled to come to terms with his emerging sexuality. Attempts at relationships with girls came to nothing, and after leaving high school he began to experiment with the Indianapolis gay community.

Good-looking and muscular thanks to a passion for bodybuilding, by his early twenties Eyler had become a well-known figure in the Indianapolis scene – though his proclivities were not to everyone's taste. Former casual partners later claimed that during sex he rarely made eye contact, and often shouted abuse and profanities.

What began as verbal abuse soon became physical, with Eyler restraining and hitting his lovers, before inflicting small cuts to their torsos with a knife, all as part of the sexual act. Psychological profiles have since suggested that the lack of eye contact, the verbal abuse and the physical attacks were all manifestations of Eyler's hatred of his own homosexuality.

By the mid-1970s he had nonetheless settled into a steady relationship with a 38-year-old Indiana State University science professor named Robert Little, and all but moved into Little's home in Terre Haute. Although the two men lived together – and often shared partners picked up by Eyler from gay bars in Indianapolis – their relationship was mostly platonic, with Little, some 15 years his senior, effectively acting as a father figure.

Given Eyler's growing taste for the more extreme end of sadomasochism, was his attack on the hitchhiker in 1978 nothing more than a sex game gone wrong, or a first experiment in what it might feel like to take that sadistic impulse to its ultimate conclusion? Whatever the truth, his narrow escape from a lengthy prison sentence (not to mention the $2,500 it cost him) taught him one thing at least: if such a situation was to happen again, he would not make the mistake of leaving the man alive.

Nevertheless, it took until October 1982 – over four years after that attack – before he claimed his first victim. But once he started, Larry Eyler did not stop.

The first to be murdered was Steven Crockett. The beaten and mutilated body of the 19-year-old was discovered in a cornfield outside Kankakee, Illinois, 40 miles south of Chicago, on 23 October 1982. He had been stabbed 32 times, mostly to the torso, with an additional four knife wounds to his head. After killing him, Eyler had made little attempt to hide the corpse.

By the time he killed Crockett, Eyler had begun a second relationship, even more bizarre than his domestic arrangement with Robert Little. John Dobrovolskis was nearly a decade younger than him and married with children, but his wife was happy to share her husband with Eyler – and even for Eyler to live with them during the week at their Chicago home, so long as he helped with the rent.

If Eyler's relationship with Little was mostly platonic, with Dobrovolskis he could give his sadomasochism free rein – the married man enjoyed being tied and beaten as much as Eyler took pleasure in hurting him. Despite this, Eyler's childhood insecurities and fear of abandonment meant he was also prone to extreme bouts of jealousy; his accusations of infidelity would lead to furious arguments in which their sexual roles were reversed, and Dobrovolskis would strike him while he did not retaliate.

The new living arrangements also meant that Eyler became a regular commuter between Terre Haute, where he spent weekends with Little, and Chicago, where he lived the rest of the week, working as a house painter. At least twice a week he would travel the 180 miles between the cities, driving alone along the highways of Indiana and Illinois, with only the occasional hitchhiker for company.

*

Despite the extreme brutality of his murder, the death of Steven Crockett did not yield any leads – and two months later, when another body was found, police were once again at a loss. John Johnson, a 25-year-old bartender from the run-down Uptown district of Chicago, had disappeared in the weeks after Crockett was killed: he was found in a field near Lowell, Indiana, on Christmas Day 1982. He too had been beaten and stabbed dozens of times, before being abandoned off Route 41, the road that leads directly from Chicago to Terre Haute.

John Johnson was the second of Eyler's victims to be found, but the third to be killed: just a week after killing Steven Crockett, Eyler had abducted and murdered 26-year-old Edgar Underkofler. His body was not discovered until the following March, again seemingly tossed aside near the town of Danville, Illinois, 60 miles north of Terre Haute on the road to Chicago. Most mystifyingly to police, his shoes and socks had been replaced with a new pair of white tube socks.

A fourth victim, 19-year-old William Lewis, had been picked up hitchhiking south of Terre Haute in November, and dumped in a field 60 miles south of Chicago. He would not be discovered for another year.

In the four weeks since killing Steven Crockett, Eyler had stabbed to death another three young men; before the end of

December he would add a further three bodies to his grisly tally.

Steven Agan, 23, and John Roach, 21, were both found on 28 December – Agan in woodland close to Route 63 around 30 miles north of Terre Haute, Roach on the side of I-70, 50 miles east of Terre Haute. Both had been stabbed, slashed and mutilated; in Steven Agan's case the wounds to his abdomen were so severe that parts of his intestines had spilled out. He too was found wearing white tube socks that his parents insisted he did not own.

Despite the sudden spate of young male murder victims along the main highways around Terre Haute and Chicago, the police still failed to connect the murders. In the early 1980s, before centralized computer databases, police departments from different states – and even different counties – had no quick and easy way to share information. Unless an officer were to actually phone around colleagues in neighbouring departments, a killer might operate across state and county lines without anyone ever thinking to look for similar cases elsewhere.

Following the discovery of Agan and Roach's corpses, however, one such opportunity to make that connection fell into the lap of the police – and, tragically, they chose to ignore it.

Despite the bodies turning up in different counties, both were sent to the same hospital for post-mortem examination. As luck would have it, the forensic pathologist on duty that day conducted both autopsies one immediately after the other.

He could not fail to notice the similarities in their injuries – especially the ferocity behind the wounds to their chests and throats – describing the attacks in his report as having been carried out with 'tremendous rage'. He also expressed the strong suspicion that both killings were the work of one man, and that there were almost certainly more victims.

His concerns fell on deaf ears: the police dismissed the idea without bothering to check with colleagues across Indiana or Illinois.

Two days later Larry Eyler killed for a seventh time. Twenty-two-year-old David Block was reported missing on 30 December after visiting his parents in Chicago. It would take until May 1984 before his remains – by then little more than a skeleton – were found, dumped in a shallow grave off Route 173, 50 miles north of Chicago.

And still, with police treating each murder as a separate investigation, the killings continued unchecked.

Larry Eyler began 1983 in a similar manner to which he had ended 1982, abducting and murdering 16-year-old Ervin Gibson on 24 January in Lake County, north of Chicago. Gibson's body lay rotting near the exit ramps for Interstate Highway 94 until 15 April – by which time Eyler had killed a further five times in five weeks. John Bartlett, Michael Bauer, Richard Wayne Jr, Jay Reynolds and Gustavo Herrera were all aged between 17 and 29. Once again, all had been subjected to frenzied knife attacks and dumped close to major highways.

With his tally now at 13, Eyler's mutilations were getting more vicious: when Gustavo Herrera's remains were found on

8 April, his right hand was missing, hacked off and thrown away by his killer.

The police may have been at a loss – but Chicago and Indianapolis's gay communities were already taking positive action against what they believed to be a serial killer targeting gay men across the two states. Memories of John Wayne Gacy, the Chicago man who had abducted and murdered at least 33 young men and boys in the late 1970s and had only been convicted a few years earlier, were still frighteningly fresh, and as early as January 1983 an anonymous tip line – complete with a reward for information leading to the killer's arrest – had been set up by *The Works*, an Indianapolis gay newspaper, accompanied by a psychological profile that described the killer as a 'self-loathing homosexual'.

The apparent motive behind the murders was further complicated by the fact that although the victims were often discovered naked, or with their trousers and underwear pulled down around their ankles, there was little (and often no) evidence of sexual assault. The self-loathing was so extreme, it seemed, that he would kill instead of having sex, rather than as part of the act.

On 9 May 1983, another two bodies surfaced – and, finally, the connection was officially made. Jimmie Roberts, 18, and Daniel McNeive, 21, had been murdered days apart, but were discovered within hours of each other – one in Cook County, Illinois, the other in Hendricks County, Indiana. As luck would have it, McNeive's autopsy was performed by the same forensic pathologist who had examined Steven Agan and John

Roach five months earlier: when he saw the 27 stab wounds across McNeive's torso – one so severe it had ripped out some of his entrails – he immediately contacted the police again.

This time they listened. Finally, officially, a hunt for a serial killer was on.

*

Six days later, a task force was put together. The Central Indiana Multi-Agency Investigation Team was originally comprised of officers from four jurisdictions across the state – but after the Team contacted the FBI's National Crime Information Center, the hunt was expanded as the scale of the killer's crimes began to become apparent. Links between victims across Indiana, Illinois and, in Jay Reynolds' case, Kentucky, now became apparent: 10 known victims had been discovered in a little under eight months, and all the signs were that there were more bodies yet to be found.

A confidential hotline was set up and in June the FBI put together their own psychological profile of their target. In an uncanny echo of the description given in *The Works* newspaper months earlier, it too predicted him to be a man living in a state of mental torment over his sexuality and whose murders were a physical manifestation of the hatred he felt towards men he was attracted to – even to the extent of punishing them for his desires. The profile also suggested that he may have had an accomplice for several of his murders, and that his partner would be older, middle class and well educated.

On 6 June, the tip line got a hit. A man named Thomas Henderson called to say that a former lover, and regular face in the Chicago gay scene, was known to favour heavy bondage – often with a knife – and, according to rumour, had previously been arrested for attacking a young man in Terre Haute. His name: Larry Eyler.

When detectives ran a background check, Eyler's 1978 stabbing and subsequent release without charge came up. It was a lead ... but it wasn't enough to bring him in. Eyler was labelled a person of interest, and placed under light surveillance.

Meanwhile, he continued to kill. Richard Bruce Jr had been picked up hitchhiking near Terre Haute on 18 May, handcuffed, stabbed and his body left by I-70, where it wouldn't be discovered until December. On 2 July, the half-naked body of a Hispanic man in his early twenties was found in a field outside the town of Paxton, Illinois, halfway between Terre Haute and Chicago. He had suffered horrific stab wounds to his abdomen and torso, but despite all efforts, he remains unidentified to this day.

The following month another body emerged. On 31 August, the mutilated corpse of 28-year-old Ralph Calise was discovered in Lake Forest, close to the sites where Ervin Gibson and Gustavo Herrera had been murdered. Like the other victims, he was shirtless, his trousers had been pulled down, there were handcuff welt marks on his wrists, and he had been stabbed at least 17 times with such ferocity that he had been partially disembowelled.

Five weeks later the body of Eric Hansen, an 18-year-old boy from Kenosha, Wisconsin, was found just over the Illinois state border, 60 miles north of Chicago. He had been extensively and repeatedly stabbed, before being decapitated and his arms and legs cut off with a hacksaw. By the time he was discovered, Larry Eyler had already been arrested.

*

When Eyler was picked up near Lowell, Indiana, on 30 September 1983, it was not on a charge connected with any of the murders. His truck had been spotted illegally parked by the highway – when a state trooper investigated, he encountered Eyler and a younger man emerging from the woods, and brought them in for questioning on charges of soliciting for sexual purposes.

Once Eyler was under caution, investigators from the task force took over. A search of Eyler's car – and subsequently of the apartment he shared with Robert Little – turned up a wealth of incriminating evidence. In his car was a makeshift armoury, including a blood-stained knife, handcuffs, a hammer, two baseball bats, a mallet, and lengths of rope and surgical tape; at the Terre Haute home he shared with Robert Little were receipts, bills and telephone records that placed him close to the murder scenes on the dates of the killings. Additionally, tyre tracks from his car and the imprints of his boots matched those found near the body of Ralph Calise.

It was enough. Eyler was charged with the murder of Ralph Calise on 29 October, bail set for $1 million and a trial date scheduled for 19 December 1983.

Finally, it seemed, police had got their man. But what happened next is almost beyond belief.

Before Eyler could face trial for murder, his lawyer set in place a series of legal challenges concerning his initial parking violation arrest. In February 1984 a judge ruled that this charge had not been enough to detain him – and that consequently the searches of the car and apartment, and the examination of the imprints of his boots that followed, were in violation of his legal rights. All of the evidence gathered as a result of those searches had to be thrown out. Suddenly there was nothing to link Eyler to the murder of Ralph Calise. Incredibly, police had to let him go.

Whether his release was the result of police bungling or down to an exceptionally smart lawyer, the grim consequence was the same. One more young man would die in agony before justice was served.

*

Following his release, Eyler moved into a new apartment in Chicago, with the rent paid by Robert Little. And for six months at least, perhaps mindful that he was now firmly on the police radar, the killings ceased.

All that changed on 19 August 1984. That night, Eyler brought home a 19-year-old male prostitute named Daniel Bridges, whom he had picked up in Uptown, Chicago. After tying him to a chair, Eyler set about inflicting the most leisurely, and most brutal, of all his killings. First beating Bridges to a pulp, he then took his time torturing him, inflicting countless knife slashes across his torso and face and hammering him with an ice pick, before stabbing him to death in a final frenzied attack that pierced his lungs and heart, as well as ripping open his intestines.

Afterwards he dragged the body into the bathroom and calmly cut it into eight pieces with a hacksaw, drained the blood, and placed the parts into six separate plastic bags. The following day he took the bags down to the communal dumpsters – where he was seen by a janitor heaving them into the trash.

In the end it was mere luck that caught Larry Eyler. On 21 August, that same janitor was preparing the dumpsters for the weekly landfill pick-up; as he shifted the bags to make room for more, one split open, and a human leg spilled out.

Police raided Eyler's apartment that same morning, surprising the killer in bed with Dobrovolskis. When a search of the property was made (properly conducted this time), huge amounts of Daniel Bridges' blood were found, as well as his clothes, and a hacksaw.

On 9 July 1986, Larry Eyler was convicted of the aggravated kidnapping, unlawful restraint and murder of Daniel Bridges and was sentenced to death. The following December he confessed to the murder of Steven Agan, though, in one final twist, he insisted he had an accomplice in that killing: his older, middle-class, well-educated father figure, Robert Little.

Little was ultimately acquitted of murder, and on 6 March 1994, Larry Eyler died of AIDS-related complications while on death row. Ten days after Eyler's death his lawyer revealed his posthumous confession to the murders of nineteen other young men and boys in addition to the two for which he had been convicted.

8

THE GOLDEN STATE KILLER: JOSEPH JAMES DEANGELO JR

(1975–86, 13+ VICTIMS)

On 18 March 1978, Bob and Gay Hardwick were asleep in their home in the northern California city of Stockton, when both were suddenly woken by a bright light shining in their eyes. Half blinded and squinting, uncertain if they were still dreaming, they froze. Behind the torch stood a powerful-looking figure in a ski mask and dark jacket; in his free hand he held a knife and a bundle of shoelaces.

Before the couple could react, he was on top of them: Bob

Hardwick struggled but was quickly overpowered, forced onto his front, tied up, gagged and left on the bed. Gay Hardwick was similarly trussed up, before their attacker calmly strolled from the bedroom and headed towards the kitchen. When he returned, it was with a pile of dishes. Stacking them carefully on Bob's back, he hissed instructions into his ear. Stay perfectly still: if he heard a single plate fall, he would kill the pair of them.

With Bob helpless, he then dragged Gay into the living room and blindfolded her. For the next few hours she was repeatedly and brutally raped, the attacker pausing only to threaten her again and again – this is not the worst. Make a sound and worse will follow. Before leaving, the intruder helped himself to the contents of her fridge, made a sandwich and drank two beers.

If it was the most terrifying night of Gay and Bob Hardwick's lives, it was also, in a macabre way, one of the luckiest. Gay had become the thirty-first victim of one of California's most notorious criminals: the following year, her attacker's whispered threats would become real, as he began killing his victims.

In San Joaquin Valley they called him the Visalia Ransacker; in Sacramento and Stockton, the East Area Rapist. In Santa Barbara, Ventura and Orange County he was the Original Night Stalker. For 12 years he terrorized California, killing at least 13 people, raping more than 50, and ransacking over 120 separate properties. He struck seemingly at random, entering his victims' homes under cover of night, spending hours indulging his darkest fantasies upon them, before disappearing again without a trace. He was headline news state-wide. Nobody was safe, not even in their own houses.

Hardware stores sold out of locks, gun ownership drastically increased, self-defence classes were oversubscribed. So prolific were the killer's crime sprees that each of them acquired their own nickname and investigating force, before decades later police finally joined the dots and realized they had in fact been carried out by the same man: a monster the media then dubbed the Golden State Killer.

For 40 years, the Golden State Killer remained at large, his identity a mystery. For 40 years his crimes stayed unsolved, a shame on law enforcement and a bogeyman to a whole generation of Californian men and women. For 40 years, nobody knew who the hell he was.

He committed his last known murder in 1986, but it was not until 15 years later that DNA technology linked the crimes. And still his identity remained a mystery – until 2018, following some of the most innovative detective work in the history of policing and over 30 years after he killed his final victim.

On 24 April of that year, Joseph James DeAngelo Jr, a 72-year-old ex-policeman living in a quiet suburb of Sacramento, around 90 miles north-east of San Francisco, was arrested and charged with eight counts of first degree murder with special circumstances. A few weeks later, another four counts of first degree murder were added; another murder charge would take the final body count to 13. At the time of his arrest, DeAngelo was enjoying a peaceful retirement at home with his daughter and granddaughter, and was known locally as a respected family man, with his eldest daughter even describing him as 'the perfect father'.

Once taken into custody he didn't even pretend to be innocent. 'I did all those things,' he told police. 'I destroyed all their lives. So now I've got to pay the price.'

The plague of murders and brutality carried out by Joseph James DeAngelo Jr remains one of the most terrifying in American history. And the story of how he was finally caught is, if anything, even more extraordinary.

*

The Golden State Killer began his criminal career while still a teenager, and his trajectory from petty thief and peeping Tom to multiple rapist and finally serial killer remains shocking, both in its speed and its predictability. If prowling and pantie-sniffing was effectively a gateway drug to sexual assault, then the sense of power he felt from raping his victims would soon drive him to seek the ultimate intoxication of murder.

Born in New York in 1945, DeAngelo spent his early years in Germany, where his father was stationed with the US Air Force. It was there, according to sister Rebecca, that he would regularly suffer beatings at the hand of his father – and also where, aged just nine, he is reported to have witnessed the rape of his seven-year-old sister Connie by two airmen. Both factors were to have a lasting impact on his developing personality.

After moving to California in the 1950s, DeAngelo was a troubled teenager; he developed a taste for inflicting cruelty on animals, as well as a fledgling burglary career. Breaking into houses, he would rifle through underwear drawers and steal small personal items or jewellery. Money was not the motive: the thrill was in the invasion, the violation.

These juvenile criminal activities were curtailed by the Vietnam War: after serving for two years with the Navy, DeAngelo enrolled in college and gained degrees in police science and criminal justice before, in 1973, joining the police as a burglary unit officer in the rural central California town of Exeter. The Navy had taught DeAngelo how to fight and how to kill; the police force taught him how to capture criminals – and how criminals escape capture.

While still in college, DeAngelo met, fell in love and became engaged to nursing student Bonnie Jean Colwell: she broke it off in 1971, claiming he had become abusive. He reacted by threatening her with a gun.

Two years later, he met and married Sharon Marie Huddle. They would stay together until 1991, by which time he was America's most wanted, and a murderer at least 13 times over. She would go on to say she had no idea of any of his criminal activities.

DeAngelo's position in the Exeter PD Burglary Unit was to be the perfect cover for the resumption of his teenage urges, and by March 1974 he was once again breaking into houses in the neighbouring town of Visalia.

Over the following two years, DeAngelo's burglary spree escalated into epidemic proportions: in just 20 months over 100 Visalia properties were ransacked, with multiple same-day robberies common. On 30 November 1974, he broke in to no fewer than 12 separate homes in a single night. The modus operandi would always be the same – single-storey properties were targeted, with windows used to gain entry – often unlocked, or else forced with a screwdriver. Multiple other windows would then be left open to provide different escape routes, dishes or glass bottles would be balanced against door handles as improvised alarms, and little of value would ever be stolen.

As with his teenage burglaries, DeAngelo's motives were not financial: only trinkets and small personal items would be taken, along with coins from piggy banks. Instead, he would rifle through underwear drawers, scatter clothes around and rearrange furniture. Once again, the kicks came from the invasion of somebody else's space. His break-ins were an exercise in power, rather than greed.

Such was the scale of his activities, the burglar soon acquired a nickname, and the 'Visalia Ransacker' became Exeter Burglary Unit's number-one priority. Naturally, as an investigating officer with the force, DeAngelo made sure that no worthwhile evidence was ever collected, and that no meaningful leads materialized.

If ransacking his victims' underwear drawers and violating their personal spaces was a thrill to DeAngelo, it soon began to pall. Like all addicts, he began to seek more. It would lead to his first killing.

On 11 September 1975, Claude Snelling, a journalism professor, was woken at around two in the morning by the sound of his back door swinging open. As he ran to investigate, he saw a figure in a ski mask in his drive, dragging his 16-year-old daughter Beth towards the street. Snelling yelled a challenge, and the figure turned, pulled a revolver and shot him twice. He did not survive the night, and DeAngelo fled the scene alone. Joseph James DeAngelo was now a murderer as well as a burglar – and soon he would add rapist to his rap sheet.

The Visalia Ransackings stopped abruptly in early 1976 – right around the time that DeAngelo moved 220 miles north, accepting a job in the police department in the town of Auburn, just outside California state capital, Sacramento.

Within months, northern California experienced a new crime wave: that of the East Area Rapist.

If DeAngelo had used his position as a police officer to cover up his crimes in Visalia, in Sacramento he applied his knowledge and experience to planning and executing a wave of more than 50 brutal rapes that once again escalated in ferocity and viciousness.

Neighbourhoods were carefully staked out, houses watched to identify who was at home and when. Prospective victims were repeatedly phoned weeks in advance; they would hear only silence or heavy breathing on the end of the line. DeAngelo would also covertly break in to the properties a day or two before the attack, in order to unlock windows, remove potential weapons, and plant shoelaces or twine as ligatures to use later.

Between June 1976 and July 1979, the East Area Rapist struck 50 times – often several times a week and on one occasion twice in 24 hours. At first his victims were exclusively young, single women, but after a media report in which he was branded 'weak' for only attacking lone women, he abruptly changed tactic, and stepped up the violence. Suddenly the East Area Rapist could strike anywhere, and at anyone; as if in direct response to the 'weak' accusation, he no longer sought lone women. Couples like Bob and Gay Hardwick were surprised in their beds, the man rendered helpless with dishes stacked on his back and the woman taken to another room and subjected to horrific and repeated abuse.

The attacks grew not only in ferocity but also in cruelty. DeAngelo would spend hours in his victims' homes, helping himself to food and drink, ransacking drawers, terrifying them with threats to torture and kill them. Sometimes he would pretend to leave before jumping out again to resume his assault. When he finally did go, he would sneak out, leaving them still tied up, uncertain as to whether it was another trick, taking with him an earring, cufflink or other small memento of his conquest. It could take hours before they managed to call for help.

The cruelty didn't end once he had left their homes: in many cases DeAngelo would call his victims in the days following the attacks. 'I'm going to come back,' he'd say. 'I'm going to come back and this time I'm going to kill you.'

Within months the East Area Rapist had become a local bogeyman; by June 1977, one year from his first attack and with 23 victims to his name, he was headline news. The previously peaceful, small-town vibe of Sacramento had been replaced by a culture of fear and distrust. Sales of locks and weapons skyrocketed; improvised vigilante groups began patrolling previously safe neighbourhoods.

DeAngelo had also begun taunting the very same police force he was a part of. 'I'm the East Side [sic] Rapist and I have my next victim already stalked and you guys can't catch me,' he said in one phone call to police. 'You are never going to catch me, East Area Rapist, you dumb fuckers,' he said in another. 'I am going to fuck again tonight. Careful!'

And still the police had no leads.

And then, in 1979, something extraordinary happened – a missed opportunity by Sacramento police that could have ended the career of the Golden State Killer even before the violence escalated into serial murder. In July of that year, Joseph James DeAngelo was kicked off the police force, after being caught shoplifting a hammer and dog repellent. As if stealing such items in the midst of a 50-rape crime wave wasn't suspicious enough, a few weeks after DeAngelo's dismissal, a prowler was spotted at the chief of police's home, peering through his daughter's bedroom window. Although the chief later said he strongly suspected it to be a vengeful DeAngelo, he never investigated further. Incredibly, the case was dropped.

Just weeks later, DeAngelo moved again, 400 miles south to Santa Barbara, a short hop up the coast from Los Angeles. At a stroke, the East Area Rapist's activities stopped – but the Santa Barbara killings began. Prowling had led to burglary, and burglary to rape, and now rape inevitably, it seemed, led to murder.

*

If DeAngelo had been shockingly prolific in his previous guises as the Visalia Ransacker and the East Area Rapist, once he intensified his activities to that of a dedicated killer, he struck more deliberately.

Despite this, however, his first intended victims escaped alive. On 1 October 1979, DeAngelo broke into a house in Goleta, Santa Barbara, and following his usual modus operandi, tied up the couple. Before he could gag them, however, and perhaps aware of the East Area Rapist's reputation, the woman screamed. The noise alerted a neighbour, who just happened to be an FBI agent: as he responded to the noise, DeAngelo fled.

He would not make a similar mistake again. Two months later, the bodies of Debra Manning and her boyfriend Robert Offerman were found in their Goleta home. Both had their wrists tied with twine – though Robert's binds were broken – and both had been shot, Debra once in the back of the head, Robert three times in the back and chest. Nothing of value had been stolen, and friends reported that Debra had expressed worries in the days before the murder that she was being followed.

On 13 March 1980, DeAngelo struck again, this time in Ventura, some 30 miles down the coast. Following his tried-and-tested routine, he had broken into the single-storey home of Charlene and Lyman Smith, surprised the couple in their bed and, after tying and gagging them, repeatedly raped Charlene, while Lyman lay helpless in another room. The difference was that now he had no intention of leaving anyone behind alive.

Perhaps mindful of the noise a gun might make, DeAngelo's

murder weapon this time was a log taken from a woodpile at the side of the house: both victims had been bludgeoned to death. In a horrific twist, their bodies were discovered three days later by Lyman's 12-year-old son from a previous marriage – he found his father and stepmother lying in pools of their own blood, wrists and ankles bound with drapery cord.

The brutality and apparent randomness of the murders led the press to declare them the work of a serial killer and they gave DeAngelo what would be his third title: the Original Night Stalker.

For his next slayings, DeAngelo travelled further south, some 150 miles from Santa Barbara to Orange County. The bodies of Patrice and Keith Harrington, a couple in their twenties who had been married for only three months, were discovered by Keith's father two days after they were killed on 19 August 1980. They had been placed next to each other under the covers of their bed, as if sleeping.

In an interview with an October 1988 issue of *Orange Coast Magazine*, Keith's father described the scene:

'Keith was there, lying on his stomach with his head turned to the left, and he was all purple and had obviously been dead for a couple of days. I pulled down the bedspread on the other side and Patti was lying on her stomach and looking in the same direction that Keith was . . . Patti was a bloody mess, the pillow was a mess bloodwise.'

Once again, DeAngelo had bludgeoned his victims to death; once again the murders were apparently completely random and utterly motiveless.

Six months later, on 6 February 1981, the Original Night Stalker returned to Orange County. Twenty-eight-year-old Manuela Witthuhn was alone in her Irvine home at the time of the attack – although she was married, her husband was in hospital with a viral infection. DeAngelo had selected her carefully: for hours he watched the house from the shadows of the yard next door until he saw the lights in the bedroom finally go out; then he crept into the backyard and prised open the rear door with a screwdriver.

The first Manuela knew of the intruder was when he jumped on her in bed, put the screwdriver to her throat and threatened to kill her if she made a sound.

Manuela stayed silent – but he killed her anyway. Her body was found the next morning by her mother; she had been repeatedly and aggressively raped, there were ligature bruise marks on her wrists and ankles, and she had been beaten to death. A few small items of jewellery had been taken and a television was missing – later found in the yard – but police quickly dismissed the idea of a botched robbery. As with the Harringtons and the Smiths, as with Debra Manning and Robert Offerman, this was clearly not the spontaneous act of a surprised burglar. This was planned, premeditated and sadistic. This was murder for the love of killing.

And still, despite the unusual knots used to bind his victims being the same as those in the East Area Rapist cases, police failed to make the connection between the activities of the Original Night Stalker and the epidemic of rape attacks in Sacramento just a few years earlier: unless Orange County and

Santa Barbara police directly and personally reached out to their colleagues in Sacramento, there was no reason for them to know the details of any of their investigations. In some instances, even the Original Night Stalker killings remained initially unlinked by detectives, with the victims' friends, colleagues and relatives all falling under suspicion instead.

Five months later, the Original Night Stalker returned to Goleta.

On the night of 27 July 1981, several residents in Goleta noticed a man loitering a few blocks from the scene of the Original Night Stalker's first killings, but despite their suspicions, nobody raised the alarm. And shortly after 3am, after hours watching a house occupied by 35-year-old single mother of two Cheri Domingo, DeAngelo prised open her bathroom window and crept inside.

He knew that Cheri would not be alone – he had seen her ex-boyfriend Gregory Sanchez enter and not leave – but he remained unconcerned. The East Area Rapist and Original Night Stalker had dealt with dozens of couples before; he had a foolproof routine.

This time, however, things did not go according to the usual script. The couple were not asleep – and at least one of them fought back. Gregory Sanchez was a powerfully built, 6-foot 3-inch, 27-year-old; and before DeAngelo could tie his wrists he made a lunge for the attacker.

How much damage Gregory inflicted is unknown, but he paid for his courage with his life. DeAngelo shot him in the face, before bludgeoning him with a garden tool. Enraged, he then turned his attention to Cheri: the following day she was found beaten to a pulp, and, as with his previous female victims, the subject of repeated rapes. Her wrists and ankles were unbound, though bruised; beside the bed was a length of shipping twine.

DeAngelo had murdered nine times – along with another two attempted killings – in just three years. And then it all went quiet. The Original Night Stalker would strike only one more time, and he waited five full years to do it.

What prompted DeAngelo to suddenly pause his campaign of terror after July 1981? Some believe that the births of his daughters during this period either left him with little free time, or else prompted a kind of reassessment of his life, while others have a more practical theory.

Retired detective Paul Holes, the former lead investigator in the Golden State Killer case, told ABC's *20/20* show in 2018 that the confrontation with Gregory Sanchez might have scared the serial killer.

'I believe what ended up happening were two things,' he said. 'In 1981, he ends up going to kill Gregory Sanchez and Cheri Domingo. And he gets in a physical fight with six-foot-three Gregory Sanchez. And I think that physical altercation with Sanchez scared him. We don't have an attack for five years.

'At this point he's an ageing offender. And so he's no longer in that prime where he's now going out as frequently as he wants, naturally due to his age. But then . . . for some reason he runs across beautiful Janelle Cruz and can't help himself.'

Janelle Cruz was to become the final – and the youngest –

victim of the Original Night Stalker, five years after his last killings. The vivacious, popular and beautiful 18-year-old was home alone in Irvine, Orange County, when, on 4 May 1986, DeAngelo entered the house through an unlocked door shortly before midnight, surprised her in the kitchen, and after binding her wrists and gagging her with a bath towel, raped and bludgeoned her to death, most likely with a pipe wrench that was later reported missing.

The Original Night Stalker was back – and the wave of murders that had terrorized southern California for three years in the early 1980s was to resume, it seemed.

Except that he was not, and it did not. DeAngelo not only apparently never killed again, it appears he never raped, ransacked, prowled or even peeped again. And as he disappeared from the radar, his taunting prophecy to Sacramento police back in 1977 took on an eerie resonance: 'You are never going to catch me, you dumb fuckers.'

*

For 32 years, that prophecy stuck. The escalating crime waves carried out by the Visalia Ransacker, East Area Rapist and Original Night Stalker not only stayed unsolved cases, but remained separate and unconnected.

Despite the scale and frequency of DeAngelo's crimes – breaking in to some 120 properties and committing at least 50 rapes and 11 known murders in just 12 years (even accounting for the five-year hiatus between 1981 and 1986) – he had also been meticulously careful to cover his tracks. As a former burglary unit officer, he knew the value of physical evidence, and acted accordingly. He always wore gloves and a ski mask – usually buying a new mask for each attack – and changed his sneakers regularly, meaning that detectives had no fingerprints, shoeprints or other identifying marks to work with. After the murders of Charlene and Lyman Smith he removed the bindings from his victims' wrists and ankles before he left the scene, perhaps mindful of police recognizing the knots he had used in his Sacramento attacks. His targeted houses were watched carefully, his quarries stalked for weeks to ensure he knew exactly what to expect from them – and similar care was put into planning escape routes, with exit points prepared in several different directions.

It took until 2001 before anyone linked the East Area Rapist and Original Night Stalker cases, and until 2016, four decades since DeAngelo's transformation from ransacker to rapist, that advances in DNA technology meant that detectives could definitively say that all of the crimes were the work of one man. It was at this point he was given a new, all-encompassing title: the Golden State Killer.

A problem persisted – whoever the Golden State Killer actually was still remained a mystery. The DNA samples may have connected the crimes, but they drew no matches on any of America's criminal databases. Perversely, one of the most notorious and feared killers in Californian history also had a record clean enough to mean he had never been swabbed.

And then, in 2017, investigators had a brainwave. Led by detective Paul Hole and FBI lawyer Steve Kramer, they uploaded their unknown killer's DNA profile to a website called GEDmatch, a 'consumer genetics' database used by ordinary citizens researching their family trees or genetic ancestries.

The website gave them the only true lead detectives had had in 40 years: around 20 people who had the same great-great-great grandparents as the Golden State Killer. From that list they were able to reconstruct family trees, and begin the meticulous process of identifying, investigating and eliminating the resulting thousands of potential suspects with shared DNA.

By early 2018 they had narrowed the list down to two. By April, just a single name: Joseph James DeAngelo Jr, then 72 years old, and living in Sacramento with his daughter and granddaughter. And only one thing remained in order to prove his guilt conclusively.

On 18 April, detectives staking out DeAngelo's home covertly collected samples of his DNA – one from the door handle of his car, another from a tissue in his garbage bin. After testing, there was no doubt. DeAngelo was a perfect match. Finally, police had their man – and on 24 April 2018 the Golden State Killer was arrested by Sacramento County Sheriff's deputies. He told officers, 'I did all those things . . . so now I've got to pay the price.'

*

DeAngelo also admitted to another two killings – the apparently random shootings of Brian and Katie Maggiore as they walked their dog in Sacramento on 2 February 1978. In exchange for a deal that meant he would avoid the death penalty, he pleaded guilty to all 13 murders, as well as 13 counts of kidnapping. He could not be charged with any of the rapes as the statute of limitations had expired for those offences, but at a special hearing before sentencing, many of those 50 victims were given an opportunity to read impact statements to him.

On 21 August 2020, aged 74, Joseph James DeAngelo was sentenced to life in prison without the possibility of parole. At the time of writing he is incarcerated at California State Prison, Corcoran, just 30 miles from his original criminal domain of Visalia.

One mystery still remains. Why, after such a vicious and prolific campaign of terror, did the Golden State Killer stop so abruptly after murdering Janelle Cruz in 1986?

Perhaps he didn't.

'Does that mean that there are not other crimes out there?' Anne Marie Schubert, Sacramento County District Attorney, told a press conference after his sentencing. 'Absolutely not. I don't believe we will ever know the magnitude of what Mr DeAngelo did.'

9

SAMUEL LITTLE

(USA, 1970–2005, 93 VICTIMS)

The forecourt of the abandoned garage made for the perfect spot to practise soccer skills. Most weekends or afternoons after school, at least one or two of the younger kids of this part of South Central Los Angeles – those not old enough to hang out with the older boys, and too broke for the games arcades or the 7-Eleven – could be found there, kicking a ball against the concrete and brick, trapping it, kicking it back, over and over again. Occasionally a misdirected shot would send the ball through one of the empty windows – the glass long since smashed – and, plucking up the courage to enter the building itself, one of them would go scampering after it, fast as he could through the dark and the dirt.

On 3 September 1989, one nine-year-old boy was preparing to do just that when he saw something unusual in the gloom. Peering through the window frame, he made out a pair of bare women's legs. It wasn't just the nakedness that shocked him: something about their angle, their absolute stillness, seemed terribly wrong. He ran home to his parents; they called the police.

The body was identified as Guadalupe Apodaca. She was 46 years old, and naked apart from a torn yellow shirt. She had died from a seizure after being strangled – most likely while her attacker knelt on her chest. The shirt she wore had semen stains on it and under her torn fingernails was someone else's blood and skin.

A week earlier another body had been found close by. Audrey Nelson, 35, was discovered curled in a foetal position in a dumpster behind a restaurant. She too was naked from the waist down, and her body was covered in bruises, burns and welts. She had a smashed spinal bone, severe head wounds, and stomach injuries consistent with being punched hard, and repeatedly. None of those things had killed Audrey – she too had died of strangulation. Her fingernails also bore evidence of her having scratched her attacker before she died.

Both bodies were classed as homicide victims, and DNA samples were taken, but little else was done. The women were prostitutes, and ageing, lowest-level streetwalkers at that, both suffering from the effects of long-term alcohol and drug addictions. Their deaths, as far as the hard-bitten, under-pressure Los Angeles Police Deparment (LAPD) was concerned, though horrible, were no great surprise. Living as they did meant risking violence every day; coming to an early end was pretty much an inevitability, one way or another.

For 23 years, their murders remained on file, unsolved and, for the most part, forgotten about. For 23 years, Guadalupe Apodaca and Audrey Nelson were just two more women who had fallen through the cracks of conventional society and paid a terrible price for it. Their lives may have been too short and too sad, but after their deaths, few people missed them.

And yet, decades later, Guadalupe Apodaca and Audrey Nelson would together be the women who led police to one of the most important arrests in US criminal history – and the worst serial killer to have ever stalked the streets of America.

*

Samuel Little first began to fantasize about strangling women as a child.

He was born in 1940 in a small town outside Atlanta, Georgia, and, with his mother being a teenage prostitute – according to some accounts, she gave birth to him while in jail – he was raised by his grandmother on the outskirts of Cleveland, Ohio. His unsettled home life was reflected at school: he later told detectives that he started having sexual fantasies about choking before he was six years old, after getting his first erection watching his kindergarten teacher touch her neck. As an adolescent he obsessively collected true crime magazines featuring women killed by strangulation; he took to pinning pictures of the victims to his bedroom walls.

By the age of 13 his behaviour had become too disruptive for the local schools, and he was sent 140 miles away, to a teenage reformatory in Columbus, Ohio.

He was not reformed. In the 18 months he spent there, he racked up 47 disciplinary infractions. Soon enough, he would fall foul of the law.

Samuel Little's first arrest was in November 1956, after he broke into a property in Nebraska a few months after his sixteenth birthday. Following a series of other offences, in 1961 he was sentenced to three years in prison for breaking into an abandoned furniture warehouse in Ohio; while incarcerated he took up boxing – his powerful frame, fearlessness and extreme aggression made him a formidable opponent in the ring.

Those three years were to be the longest stretch Little would serve until his final arrest in 2012 – but they by no means made an honest man out of him. Between 1957 and 1975 he would be arrested 26 times across 11 different states, as he lived a shiftless, itinerant life, travelling the country, taking odd jobs and stealing what he could in order to get by. The charges over that period included shoplifting, theft, driving under the influence, fraud, breaking and entering, and the solicitation of a prostitute.

By 1976, the petty theft and burglary had escalated into violence. In September he was charged with the rape, assault and robbery of a woman in Missouri. She had been found with her hands bound, near-hysterical, badly beaten and with her neck bruised black from strangulation. She had also been sodomized.

Little's lawyer pled the charge down to 'assault with intent to ravish', and he served just three months in county jail.

Even allowing for the benefit of hindsight, three months for assaulting, strangling and raping someone seems extraordinarily lenient – but it pales in comparison to what would happen over the following decade.

In September 1982, the naked body of 26-year-old Patricia Mount was found in a field near Gainesville, Florida. She had been killed by strangulation, and was last seen dancing with a man matching Little's description in a bar, before the pair drove off together in his brown station wagon. After hairs found on her appeared to match Little's, he was arrested, charged and tried for murder.

Little did not deny having met Patricia – and his lawyer argued that his hairs could have been transferred to her as they danced. In January 1984 a jury decided that was enough to constitute reasonable doubt – and he walked free from court.

That acquittal came almost immediately after another dismissed murder charge. In October 1982, just one month after Patricia Mount's battered body was discovered in Florida, the skeletal remains of 22-year-old Melinda LaPree were uncovered in a graveyard in the town of Pascagoula, Mississippi, some 400 miles to the west of Gainesville. She too had been strangled – and she too was last seen getting into a station wagon similar to Little's. In the course of the investigation, two prostitutes from Pascagoula claimed they had each also been assaulted and strangled by Little – but despite their statements, a grand jury declined to indict him for LaPree's murder, claiming that the lack of hard evidence and the dubious reliability of the prostitutes' statements meant securing a conviction would be unlikely.

'At that time frame, through societal ways, we just didn't believe prostitutes when they cried rape,' Lieutenant Darren Versiga of the Pascagoula PD later told the *Los Angeles Times*.

After his acquittal, Little next turned up in San Diego, California – and soon found himself in court again. In October 1984 he was arrested on charges of kidnapping, assaulting and strangling two women, both of whom survived, one by pretending to be dead as he tossed her from his car. Eventually tried for attempted murder in both cases, he once more dodged a lengthy prison sentence: after pleading guilty to the lesser charges of assault and false imprisonment, he served just two and a half years in prison.

On his release in February 1987, Little moved to Los Angeles. He would not face serious jail time again until 2012, by which time he had killed at least 60 – and as many as 93 – women.

*

How could a man rack up dozens of arrests in 11 states for crimes including assault and rape, as well as face three separate indictments for murder or attempted murder in as many years, and not be flagged up as a serious and deadly danger to society?

Whatever the failings of the justice system in Samuel Little's case, the consequences were beyond horrific. The reality was, by the time he was freed from his two-and-a-half-year sentence in 1987, he was already a murderer 31 times over.

On his release from prison he wasted no time in killing again – and would continue to do so at a terrifying rate. All of his victims were women on the very margins of society: sex workers, drug addicts, dropouts; many had no fixed address, most had no family. When their bodies were discovered, beaten, strangled and raped, the police mostly dismissed their cases as little more than the tragic, and sadly predictable, outcomes of the lives they led.

Over the following decades, Little continued his rootless, nomadic lifestyle, accumulating arrests in seven separate states across the country for crimes including theft, shoplifting, burglary, larceny and drunkenness. In the summer of 2007 he was arrested in Los Angeles for possession of cocaine. Ironically, it was this comparatively minor offence that would prove his eventual undoing.

As part of his guilty plea to the drugs charge, Little was ordered to attend a drug rehabilitation programme – and after he failed to turn up, a warrant was issued. Five years later, in September 2012, he was finally pulled in for it – picked up and arrested at a homeless shelter in Louisville, Kentucky – and extradited to Los Angeles.

This time he would not get away with a minimal jail sentence. Back in LA detectives were waiting for him with DNA evidence from a pair of murders committed 23 years earlier.

*

For over two decades, the killings of Guadalupe Apodaca and Audrey Nelson had lain dormant in the unsolved files of the LAPD. At the time of their murders, DNA profiling was still in its relative infancy, and although the genetic material found under their fingernails and on Apodaca's shirt had been logged, it would take until 2012 before the technology, and the will, existed to make a definitive match.

At some point in his long and varied criminal career, Samuel Little had undergone a DNA swab as a routine part of his being taken into custody. When detectives from a reinvigorated LAPD cold case squad once again opened the files of the two sex workers found strangled in a dumpster and an abandoned garage in South Central in 1989, they ran their DNA evidence through the national computer database. Little's name came up as a match. It was his skin under their fingernails; it was his semen on Apodaca's shirt.

When his rap sheet showed prior arrests for murder and attempted murder – all involving strangulation and sexual assault – detectives were convinced they had their man. The only question was: how many other victims might there be?

On 7 January 2013, Little was charged with the murders of Guadalupe Apodaca and Audrey Nelson, as well as of another woman, 41-year-old Carol Alford, who had been found half-naked in a South Central alleyway in July 1987, choked to death and with severe injuries to her head from punching. Little's DNA was a match for stains on her underwear and under her fingernails. The following September he was found guilty of all three murders and sentenced to spend the rest of his life behind bars.

Finally, after so many missed chances, justice had been served – but detectives were convinced it was not the end of the story. As it turned out, it was barely the beginning.

It took until 2018, by which time he was 78 years old and using a wheelchair, before Samuel Little began talking – first to a Texas Ranger named James Holland, who was investigating historic unsolved murders in that state, and then to Jillian Lauren, a true crime reporter. The story he had to tell was worse than anyone could have imagined.

In a series of separate interviews with Holland and Lauren, Little claimed that besides the three murders for which he had been convicted, he had killed another 90 women in a terrifying campaign that dated back nearly 50 years.

Lauren would write about her encounters in a book, *Behold the Monster*, in one instance describing the moment he told her about the first time he had ever killed.

"'She was a big ol' blonde,' Little said. "Round about turn of the New Year, 1969 to 1970. Miami. Coconut Grove. She was a ho." Then he corrected himself: "A prostitute. She was sitting at a restaurant booth, red leather, real nice. She crossed them big legs in her fishnet stockings and touched her neck. It was my sign. From God.'"

Little's modus operandi had been the same throughout each of his murders: targeting lonely, damaged women with the offer of drugs, alcohol, or money for sex, he would pick them up in cheap bars or hustling on the street, entice them somewhere deserted – or else simply in the back of his car – and once they were alone, stun them with a sudden flurry of fast, vicious jabs to the head, using the techniques he had learned as a boxer to knock them unconscious. He'd then take his time, stripping, raping and beating his victim, before delivering the coup de grâce – strangling them to death with one hand while masturbating with the other.

The bodies would be left without much concern for their detection, dumped in alleys, fields, abandoned buildings, dumpsters, or on one occasion tossed into the Mississippi River. When Jillian Lauren asked him why he did it, he replied: 'I wanted their helplessness. All I ever wanted was for them to cry in my arms.'

As the confessions came – often complete with drawings of his victims – so too did a huge reopening of cold murder cases across the country.

In December 2018 Little was found guilty of the 1994 murder of Denise Brothers, a 32-year-old found strangled in a vacant lot in Odessa, Texas. The following August he was convicted of another four slayings: Annie Stewart, 32, discovered in woods near Cincinnati in October 1981; Mary Jo Peyton, a 21-year-old he had picked up in a Cleveland bar in 1984, taken to a derelict factory, choked to death and then left at the bottom of a basement staircase; Zena Marie Jones, 30, a Memphis prostitute he strangled in his car and dumped in the river in July 1990; and Rose Evans, 32, whom he met in Cleveland and choked to death in August 1991, before leaving her body in a vacant lot.

Little died two years later in prison, convicted of eight murders, but still claiming his true tally was 93 victims. In the years since, the FBI have formally connected Little to 60 confirmed homicides over a period of 27 years and spanning 15 states.

Almost all of them were sex workers, drug addicts or homeless women. So cut off from the protection of 'normal' society were they that only 11 have ever been properly identified. The dozens of other victims he says he killed remain unknown to this day, their deaths either logged as accidents or overdoses . . . or else simply not noticed at all.

10

AILEEN WUORNOS

(USA, 1989–90, 7 VICTIMS)

She has been called America's first female serial killer.

According to the FBI's official definition of what constitutes a serial killer – as opposed to a mass shooter, terrorist or other multiple murderer – the perpetrator must have killed at least three people, have targeted victims previously unknown to them and who did not know each other, and have allowed some time to elapse between each murder.

Between November 1989 and November 1990 Aileen Wuornos shot to death seven men in Florida, some months apart, some days apart. All were previously strangers to her, all had picked her up soliciting for sex on the highways, all were killed by multiple gunshots. Six of their bodies were found rotting in woodland or backroads, one remains missing to this day. Each of them was robbed after their deaths.

Their killer never expressed any remorse. After her arrest, Wuornos declared in a 2001 petition to the Florida Supreme Court: 'I killed those men, robbed them as cold as ice. And I'd do it again, too. There's no chance of keeping me alive or anything, because I'd kill again. I have hate crawling through my system . . . I'm competent, sane, and I'm trying to tell the truth. I'm one who seriously hates human life and would kill again.'

Did that make Aileen Wuornos a classic predatory serial killer, driven by a dark, incomprehensible, unstoppable urge to slaughter in the manner of murderers like Dennis Nilsen and Joseph James DeAngelo, or even of couples like Fred and Rosemary West or Ian Brady and Myra Hindley?

Perhaps so. Perhaps not. Despite the callousness and ruthlessness of her crimes, despite her insistence she had 'hate crawling through my system', it's hard not to feel at least a little sympathy for Wuornos. She was a murderer seven times over, she was the FBI's very definition of a serial killer – but in a horribly real sense, she was also a victim.

*

It was almost a miracle Aileen Wuornos lived long enough to kill at all.

Born on the extra day of the leap year in February 1956 in the town of Rochester, Michigan, she barely knew her parents. Her mother, Diane Wuornos, had married her father, Leo Pittman, aged just 14, when he was 18. They divorced before Aileen was born two years later, and Leo Pittman later committed suicide in prison, where he was serving a life sentence for kidnapping and raping a seven-year-old girl.

Before Aileen was four years old, Diane abandoned her and her older brother Keith, leaving them with her parents Lauri and Britta – both children would grow up believing that these were their real parents.

If being brought into the care of their grandparents was meant to provide some structure and permanency to Aileen and Keith's young lives, it had the opposite effect. Both Lauri and Britta were alcoholics, and Aileen would later claim that her grandfather would beat and sexually abuse her, and even that he would be joined in the abuse by her brother Keith. She took the experience with her to school, bartering sexual favours in exchange for cigarettes, alcohol or drugs before she was even 11 years old. It was effectively to be the beginning of a lifelong career in prostitution.

Aged 14, Aileen became pregnant – the identity of the father was never established – and in 1971 she gave birth to a baby boy. The child was given up for adoption, and Aileen's grandfather banished her from his home.

For the next five years she lived on the streets, hitchhiking across the country, sleeping rough and scraping a living through prostitution, most often with men who would pick her up on the side of the highway. What money she made was spent getting drunk or high – anything to numb the pain and loneliness.

By 1976 her shiftless existence had taken her to Florida where, for perhaps the only time in her life, Aileen was offered a real chance at happiness and stability. Still just 20, she took up with Lewis Gratz Fell, a wealthy 69-year-old retiree who had become besotted with her. The couple were married within weeks of meeting, but rather than embrace the new beginning, it seems Aileen viewed her marriage as just another exchange of money for sex. Treating her husband with the same contempt with which she viewed the men who picked her up on the interstates for 20-minute tricks, her scorn soon turned violent: before their marriage was a month old he had taken out a restraining order against her when she beat him after he refused to give her any more money. On 21 July, after just nine weeks together, their union was annulled.

By this time Aileen didn't need him anyway. Days earlier her brother Keith had died of oesophageal cancer and, newly flush with $10,000 from his life insurance, she embarked on a wild spending spree.

The cash lasted just two months, and before the summer was over, she was back on the streets, hustling for sex and racking up arrests for petty thefts, cheque forgery, disturbing the peace, resisting arrest, and in one instance, armed robbery, in which she made off with the pathetic total of $35 and two packs of cigarettes.

It was a miserable, desperate life, and it took its toll. In 1978, still only 22 but by then already a seven-year veteran of homelessness and prostitution, she tried to put an end to it all, shooting herself in the stomach with a stolen revolver.

It was the sixth time she had attempted suicide since she was 14. Like everything else she had ever done, it was a failure, and only led to more misery and pain.

After her recovery, there was nowhere to go but back to the streets – and for another eight years, Aileen Wuornos kept up her itinerant existence across the highways of Florida, hitching lifts, turning tricks, stealing what she could, living day to day with no real hope of anything getting any better.

And then in the summer of 1986, finally, some light came into her life. Aileen Wuornos fell in love.

*

Aileen Wuornos met Tyria Moore in a Daytona bar in June 1986, and the two women hit it off immediately. For every one of her 30 years, all Aileen had known was loneliness and abuse, any sense of self-worth lost (or never developed) from decades of selling her body. Every relationship in her life had been essentially transactional – but in Tyria Moore, Aileen found someone who not only wanted nothing from her, but actually wanted to help and protect her. Most astonishingly, she found she felt the same way.

'It was love beyond imaginable,' Wuornos would later say. 'Earthly words cannot describe how I felt about Tyria.'

The couple may have been lovers, and even soulmates, but they were not about to settle down and live happily ever after. Moore's life was almost as chaotic and rootless as her own; and together the pair continued where each of them had left off, supporting themselves with low-level robberies and petty thefts, living in cheap motel rooms when they had money, or else sleeping in the woods or abandoned buildings when they did not. The bulk of their income came from Aileen's prostitution, working the Florida interstates, picking up men at truck stops or on exit ramps and hitching back from wherever she was dropped off afterwards.

Thanks to her extensive rap sheet – and especially the year she had spent in prison following her armed robbery conviction – Wuornos began using a range of aliases, either when detained by police or when checking into motels.

As 'Lori Grody' she was questioned after a man accused her of pulling a gun in his car and robbing him of $200; as 'Susan Blahovec' she and Moore were held by police on suspicion of assault and battery after a man was attacked with a beer bottle in a Daytona bar; as 'Cammie Green' she was again questioned by Daytona police after a violent altercation with a bus driver.

By 1989, the couple's situation was becoming desperate. Wuornos's dependency on alcohol was worsening, and, now 33 and with the effects of nearly 20 years living rough beginning to become all-too apparent, finding men prepared to pay to have sex with her was not as easy as it had been a decade before. Her already volatile temper became near-uncontrollable and was now married to a paranoid misanthropy (or at least misandry): her resentment of society, and men specifically, became all-consuming and she took to carrying a .22 calibre pistol in her purse wherever she went.

Men were at fault for all the problems in her life, she told

Moore. Men like her father, a paedophile who abandoned her before she was even born; men like her grandfather, who sexually abused her as a child and then kicked her out of the house as a teenager; men like Lewis Gratz Fell, who wanted her body but wouldn't give her the money she needed; men like all the countless leering, anonymous, disgusting animals who had paid her for sex one way or another since before she was 11 years old. If it wasn't for men, she said, she wouldn't be such a goddamn mess.

In the autumn of 1989 she did something about it.

*

Aileen Wuornos claimed that the first time she killed, it was in self-defence.

On 30 November 1989, Richard Mallory, a 51-year-old owner of a TV repair business, picked her up hitchhiking on the I-4 east of Orlando. As they drove, she gave him the usual proposition, and after agreeing a price, they turned off the interstate, along the backroads to a secluded, wooded area, where they would have sex.

Two days later, Mallory's car was found near Daytona. His wallet – cleaned out of cash – was nearby, along with condoms and a half-empty bottle of vodka. A month later, on 13 December, his body turned up in the woods a few miles to the north-west: he had been shot three times in the chest and his remains covered up with a piece of carpet.

Wuornos would subsequently claim that she had never

intended to kill Richard Mallory, but that after they had pulled off the road he had turned violent, beating, raping and sodomizing her – in desperation, she said, she had grabbed her pistol and shot him in self-defence.

She was never believed – though it later transpired that Mallory had form for exactly the allegations she made against him. In 1957 he had been sentenced to 10 years in a psychiatric prison after pleading insanity to attempted rape charges.

In December 1989, however, he was just another random, and apparently motiveless, shooting. Police investigating the murder were left with few leads, and before spring the trail went cold.

Whether Aileen Wuornos had killed Mallory because she genuinely feared for her own life, or as a deliberate, cold-hearted act of revenge on men in general, the bottom line was the same: she had got away with it. The money she stole from him bought her and Tyria a few more nights in a motel, and a few more rounds in the bars of Daytona.

She would not kill again for six months. But once she started, she did not stop.

On 19 May 1990, 47-year-old construction worker David Spears was reported missing, last seen leaving Sarasota on Florida's west coast, headed on the I-75 and I-4 towards Orlando. His corpse turned up on 1 June, 130 miles north in Citrus County; he was naked and had been shot six times with a .22 pistol. Two of the shots had been fired into his back, presumably as he tried to escape.

By the time Spears was discovered, Wuornos had already claimed a third victim. Charles Carskaddon, 40, was a part-time rodeo worker from Missouri who had been driving down the I-75 to meet his fiancée in Tampa. At some point he had picked up Wuornos hitchhiking – whatever else happened between them after that remains unclear, except that she shot him nine times in the chest and stomach. His badly decomposed remains were found on 6 June, 30 miles from those of David Spears, wrapped in an electric blanket.

Was it the violent encounter with Richard Mallory that turned Aileen Wuornos from victim to aggressor? Did his alleged rape of her prove the final straw for a woman who had been used and abused for as long as she could remember, tipping her already established contempt of the men who paid her for sex into an active campaign of revenge upon them? Or had decades of alcoholism, destitution and prostitution finally proved too much for an already unbalanced mind, to the point where killing simply wasn't that big a deal to her?

Either way, the bodies kept coming.

Troy Eugene Burress, a 50-year-old sausage salesman, was reported missing on 31 July; four days later, his body was discovered by a family picnicking in the Ocala National Forest, around 70 miles north-west of Orlando. He was fully dressed and had been shot twice with a .22 pistol – once in the chest, and once in the back.

The following month another middle-aged man turned up dead near Ocala. Charles 'Dick' Humphreys, 56, was a retired Air Force Major and former Alabama Chief of Police: he was found on 12 September, shot seven times and with his pockets turned inside out.

In November came a sixth body. Truck driver and reserve police officer Walter Antonio, 62, was discovered naked apart from his socks in woods 60 miles west of Gainesville. He had been shot three times in the back and once in the back of the head.

Six bodies – all men aged between 40 and 62 – had turned up in 12 months, five of them between June and November 1990. Apart from their sex and age, and the fact they had all been killed with bullets fired from a .22-calibre weapon, they appeared to have little in common. Their cars had all been stolen and then abandoned after their deaths, and what valuables they had on them, or in their vehicles, had likewise been taken. Florida police knew they were hunting either an extraordinarily heartless robber . . . or else a serial killer.

In the meantime, Tyria Moore had begun to grow increasingly concerned about her lover. While she was well used to Wuornos disappearing for hours, sometimes days, when picking up clients on the interstates and Florida freeways, through the summer of 1990 the spoils of her prostitution took a stranger turn.

Wuornos was bringing home more cash than usual, as well as jewellery to pawn. When the jewellery was joined by briefcases, toolboxes, male toiletries, watches, cameras and even fishing gear, Wuornos's insistence that she had simply stolen the bounty seemed unlikely at best.

By the time Walter Antonio's body was discovered, Moore's concern had grown into fear. Robbery, prostitution and even assault was one thing – but if her girlfriend had become a murderer, Tyria Moore wanted no part of it. That same month she told Wuornos she was leaving to see her family in Pennsylvania. Alone.

*

Florida police had six known victims of their serial killer – but there was a seventh. And it would be his murder that would help detectives to finally put a halt to Aileen Wuornos's deadly vendetta.

In June 1990, Peter Siems, a 65-year-old retired merchant seaman, had left his home in Jupiter, Florida, on a road trip to visit relatives in Arkansas. He never showed up, and on 22 June, a missing persons report was filed.

Peter Siems was never found – but his car was. On 4 July, a resident of Orange Springs, a remote rural community on the northern edge of Ocala National Forest, saw a Pontiac Sunbird come careering off the road and smash into the trees. Two women emerged, one blonde, one brunette, and fled into the woods before she could help. The car was identified as belonging to Siems, and a bloody palm print – not his – was lifted from an interior door handle.

That witness had given detailed descriptions of the women to police, and on 30 November, suspecting that the disappearance of Siems might be linked to their other six bodies, Florida authorities released composite sketches of their suspects and appealed for information.

Two names kept popping up. Tyria Moore, and Susan Blahovec.

At the same time, detectives hit the pawnshops. In Daytona they found a ring belonging to Walter Antonio and a camera formerly owned by Richard Mallory; a few miles up the coast in Ormond Beach was Richard Spears's toolbox. All had been pawned by women calling themselves Susan Blahovec, Lori Grody or Cammie Green.

By law, all Florida pawnshops are required to take a fingerprint from their customers – when detectives ran the prints of Blahovec, Grody and Green they got a single match: 34-year-old known prostitute, petty thief and convicted armed robber Aileen Wuornos. The prints also matched those taken from Peter Siems's wrecked car.

On 9 January 1991, Wuornos was tracked to a ramshackle bikers' bar called, ironically, the Last Resort, in Port Orange, a few miles from Daytona. When police arrested her, they told her she was being taken in for an outstanding warrant. The following day they found Tyria Moore – and the final wretched act of Aileen Wuornos's life unfolded.

If Wuornos's murder spree had been an unhinged revenge on men for what she saw as a lifetime of abuse and exploitation, then her final betrayal was to come at the hands of a woman, and the only person she ever loved.

Tyria Moore cut a deal with the cops. In exchange for immunity from prosecution, she would elicit a confession from her lover. Over a series of taped phone calls she begged her to come clean about the killings – until, finally, she agreed. On 16 January 1991, Wuornos told detectives: 'Well, I came here to confess to murder.'

*

A year later, on 14 January 1992, Wuornos stood trial for the murder of Richard Mallory. From her first confession she maintained that she had shot him in self-defence as he raped her; by a quirk of Florida law, however, his prior conviction for attempted rape was deemed inadmissible by the judge, and on 27 January she was found guilty. As the jury returned their verdict, Wuornos leapt from her seat: 'I'm innocent!' she screamed. 'I was raped! I hope you get raped! Scumbags of America!'

Four days later she was sentenced to death.

Aileen Wuornos would later plead no contest to the murders of Charles 'Dick' Humphreys, Troy Eugene Burress and David Spears, and guilty to the murders of Charles Carskaddon and Walter Antonio. No charges were ever brought for the killing of Peter Siems, as his body remains undiscovered.

In each case she argued that her victims were either rapists, or at least intended to rape her. 'If I didn't kill them they would have hurt someone,' she said, according to a jailer's sworn statement. 'If I didn't kill all those guys I would have been raped a total of 20 times maybe. Or killed. Sure I killed these seven guys, but they deserved it. On a killing day those guys always wanted to go way, way back in the woods. Now I know why they did it: they were gonna hurt me.'

Aileen Wuornos was executed by lethal injection on 9 October 2002. Two years later, Charlize Theron's harrowing portrayal of the killer in the movie *Monster* would win her an Academy Award for Best Actress.

If the first question any investigation into a serial killer asks is 'why?', then Aileen Wuornos's chaotic, abused, desperate and despairing life would seem to offer at least some kind of answer. There is no excusing her crimes, but perhaps there can be something like understanding.

By the end, she begged for death. For the woman who had attempted suicide six times by the age of 22, it may have been all she ever really wanted.

11

GARY RIDGWAY

(USA, 1982–2000, 49–90 VICTIMS)

Until 2018, when Samuel Little's true tally of victims became known, America's most prolific serial killer was a truck painter from Washington State. He did not murder until he was in his early thirties, but once he had claimed his first victim, he killed at a staggering rate, strangling at least 40 more young women and teenage girls in just 18 months. After his eventual arrest nearly 20 years later, he confessed to murdering almost twice that number: 22 of those bodies have never been found.

The motivations behind Gary Ridgway's murderous impulses are not difficult to unravel. He targeted prostitutes and teenage runaways; he killed them after – or sometimes while – having sex with them; he killed them because he simultaneously lusted after and despised them. In a statement read out at his trial he declared: 'I wanted to kill as many women I thought were prostitutes as I possibly could. I picked prostitutes as my victims because I hate most prostitutes and I did not want to pay them for sex . . . I picked prostitutes because I thought I could kill as many of them as I wanted without getting caught.'

For 19 years he did just that, slaughtering between 49 and 90 girls and young women near Seattle and Tacoma, Washington State, without, in many cases, anyone ever noticing they had gone missing at all. He kept the dead bodies in 'clusters', and would return to have sex with the corpses even as they lay rotting for weeks and months after. He left no evidence of his kills, he took no trophies, he told nobody. When he was finally exposed, even his wife had no idea of his secret life.

'He displayed no empathy for his victims and expressed no genuine remorse,' prosecutors said. 'He killed because he wanted to. He killed because he could. He killed to satisfy his evil and unfathomable desires.'

Ridgway himself was just as unambiguous. 'Choking is what I did,' he told investigators. 'And I was pretty good at it.'

*

In the summer of 1982, bodies began surfacing in and around the Green River, a 65-mile-long waterway that flows from the western slopes of the Cascade mountain range in Washington

State, through the forests of King County to the twin cities of Seattle and Tacoma.

First to turn up was Wendy Lee Coffield. The 16-year-old had been reported missing from her foster home on 8 July 1982 – one week later she was found floating in the water, dead from strangulation. On 12 August the naked body of Debra Bonner, 23, was discovered, slumped over a log in the Green River. She too had been choked to death.

Three days later, a fisherman chanced upon three more bodies. Marcia Chapman, 31, and Cynthia Hinds, 17, were both half-naked and pinned underwater by large rocks; close by, hidden in the trees, was the corpse of 16-year-old Opal Mills. Again, all three had been asphyxiated – though, intriguingly for investigators, post-mortem examinations revealed that they had been killed as much as 12 days apart from one another.

On 25 September, a sixth victim of the newly dubbed 'Green River Killer' was found. Seventeen-year-old Gisele Lovvorn was a prostitute who had been missing since mid-July: her naked remains were discovered in an abandoned house near Seattle-Tacoma Airport, along with a pair of men's socks used to strangle her.

By then police were already convinced there was a serial killer on the loose in King County – the fact that all the victims had been strangled, were either nude or partially naked, and shared troubled backgrounds, indicated that their deaths were not random, but part of a targeted pattern of murders.

A task force was assembled, and, given the victims' histories of prostitution, investigators turned their attention to Seattle's red light district, interviewing women who worked the main strip in an effort to gain any information on violent or choking-obsessed customers.

The interviews turned up few leads – already suspicious of the police, and well used to dealing with the daily threat of violence, they were reluctant to talk; and meanwhile, young women continued to disappear. Between mid-September 1982 and the end of April 1983, another 17 sex workers or runaways vanished, all aged between 14 and 23. The first of their bodies would turn up in January 1983, when 16-year-old Linda Jane Rule was discovered in Seattle. The last to be found, Becky Marrero, 20, would not be unearthed until December 2010, 27 years after her death.

Finally, after nine months of frustration, in early May 1983 it seemed like investigators might have caught a break. The boyfriend of Marie Malvar, an 18-year-old prostitute who had disappeared on 30 April, reported seeing her arguing with a customer as they sped away in his truck that night. The week afterwards, he spotted the truck again, and after following it to a house in the Tacoma area, called the police.

When detectives questioned the owner, a twice-divorced 34-year-old truck painter, he denied ever having met Malvar. With nothing but the boyfriend's word for it, the matter was considered closed. Had they bothered to run a background check on the truck driver, they would have discovered a prior arrest for allegedly choking a prostitute three years earlier – pleading self-defence, he had been released from custody without charge.

Before the month was out, another four teenage girls and a 21-year-old woman would meet their ends at the hands of the Green River Killer.

*

Sex had dominated Gary Ridgway's life since he was a child.

Born the second of three sons to Thomas and Mary Ridgway in Salt Lake City, Utah, in 1949, Gary was an insecure child with an IQ rated 'low average', and suffered from a bedwetting problem until his early teens. The humiliation of this condition was compounded by his mother's bizarre insistence on bathing his genitals herself after every incident.

Ridgway later told forensic psychologists that the practice provoked confusing feelings: the impressionable teenager felt simultaneously sexually attracted to his mother, while hating her for 'making' him feel a way that he knew was wrong. According to psychologist Reid Meloy, the seeds of his later killings were sown during the shame of these night-time ablutions.

'For an adolescent, having your mother wash your genitals would be highly exciting and arousing, but it would also be humiliating,' Meloy told the *Washington Post* in a November 2003 article. 'With humiliation would come rage towards the mother. That is very common in serial murderers – displaced matricide. Unconsciously, he is killing his mother over and over again.'

Gary's adolescent view of sex was to be confused still further by his father Thomas. By this time the Ridgways had moved to a run-down part of the Seattle-Tacoma area of Washington; sex workers were a common sight on the streets around their home, and the family would often be subjected to long rants by Thomas about the bad influence the presence of prostitutes and their clients could have on his children.

The overall effect on the teenager was profound. As Gary Ridgway grew up, he became simultaneously obsessed with and shamed by sex, as well as both fascinated and repulsed by those who sold it.

Two of his marriages were to fall victim to this obsession. His first, to childhood sweetheart Claudia Kraig, when he was 20 and she just 19, ended after a year due to his repeated infidelities – often with sex workers – and his second, to Marcia Winslow, despite lasting eight years and resulting in a son, also ended the same way. Both women subsequently described his insatiable sexual appetite: as well as wanting to have sex several times a day, he would encourage them to do so in public places, and in increasingly unusual ways. Winslow claimed that on one occasion this included placing her in a chokehold.

It was during his second marriage that Ridgway also developed a fervent passion for religion, not only attending church, but reading the Bible aloud at home and work, and even canvassing the neighbourhood, attempting to convert non-believers door-to-door . . . all while continuing to indulge his sexual desires with an often-unwilling Winslow, or else with the same prostitutes he so loudly denounced as sinners.

That marriage ended in 1981; the following year he began killing.

*

When detectives following up the Marie Malvar lead questioned – and then discounted – Gary Ridgway, he had already killed 25 times.

His modus operandi was nothing if not consistent. Prowling the Seattle strip in his truck, he would pick up a girl or young woman on the pretext of paying them for sex. Some of these were experienced sex workers; others teenage runaways desperate for cash; others still may not have offered any services, but simply had the look to Ridgway of the kind of girl who might sell her body.

Once in his truck he would drive somewhere remote, and kill them, often while having sex, strangling them from behind, most often with his bare hands, other times with improvised ligatures such as a shoelace. The bodies would be left, nude or half-naked, in what he later described as 'clusters'.

'I placed most of the bodies in groups which I call clusters,' he said in his confession. 'I did this because I wanted to keep track of all the women I killed. I liked to drive by the clusters around the county and think about the women I placed there.'

He did not only like to think about them – he would also return to his clusters to have sex with the corpses, claiming that it was not from a love of necrophilia, but because doing so would delay the need to find another living victim, and so lessen his chances of getting caught.

He was also meticulous about covering his tracks. Prostitutes were targeted because of his lifelong love–hate relationship with sex workers, but also because their disappearance was less likely to be noticed, or cared about. Despite his below-average IQ, he showed a keen understanding of forensic evidence: he always wore gloves, changed the tyres of his truck regularly, and carefully clipped the nails of each of his victims after their deaths, just in case they had scratched him. He would also strip them of any jewellery to make identification harder – and rather than risk pawning the items, would leave them in gas station restrooms for other women to take away. As he grew in confidence he took to planting false evidence around the bodies, such as cigarette butts or chewing gum wrappers, despite the fact he did not smoke or chew gum.

By the beginning of May 1983, Ridgway may have killed 25 times, but so far only eight bodies had turned up. That was to change over the summer. In August, the remains of 16-year-old Shawnda Leea Summers were uncovered near SeaTac Airport – she had been missing since the previous October. A month later, Gail Lynn Mathews, 23, missing since April, was found in the Star Lake area of Tacoma, and in October three more victims surfaced.

Yvonne Antosh, 19, Constance Naon, 19, and Kelly Marie Ware, 22, had all disappeared from Seattle the previous summer – their remains were discovered within two weeks of each other. Eighteen-year-old Mary Meehan followed in November, and 16-year-old Kimi-Kai Pitsor on 15 December 1983. All had been raped, all had been strangled.

Even as police recovered the bodies, Ridgway kept killing: in the same period, another 16 young women and teenage girls went missing. It would take until 2003 before the last of their remains were found.

In the year and a half since Wendy Coffield had been found floating in the Green River, the police had 15 confirmed victims of the Green River Killer – but also more than twice as many additional young women reported missing in the same time frame.

Although the bodies kept coming – another 11 victims would be discovered in 1984 – after the rampage of killing that saw Ridgway strangle 41 women at a rate of roughly one every 12 days through 1982 and 1983, he suddenly slowed down dramatically.

After he killed his last victim of 1983, 19-year-old Lisa Yates, whom he choked to death on 23 December, Ridgway only accounted for two known deaths in 1984, one in 1986 and one again in 1987 and 1990, and then did not strike again until 1998.

Why? On the one hand, he had fallen in love, with Judith Mawson, whom he was to wed in 1988 and would remain married to until his eventual arrest 13 years later. In subsequent interviews, Ridgway said that he truly loved her – it might be that he had finally found someone who satisfied his sexual appetites to the extent that he simply didn't need to kill. For her part, she claimed to have no idea that her besotted husband was America's most prolific serial killer.

On the other hand, it was during the mid-1980s that Ridgway finally fell under suspicion by police investigating the Green River murders. In 1984 he was questioned after his description matched that given by a witness who had seen one of the victims being picked up by a man driving a similar truck to his before she disappeared. Brought in for questioning, he denied everything – and even offered to take a polygraph test to prove his innocence.

Astonishingly, for a man of such supposed low IQ, he passed, and, once again, was released.

Investigators may not have been able to hold Ridgway, but to have a couple of separate witnesses link him to the disappearances of two of the Green River Killer's victims was too much of a coincidence to ignore. From now on, he was firmly on their radar. It may be that, aware of their scrutiny, after his second questioning he managed to exercise more control over his murderous urges.

As detectives looked closer at Ridgway's background and activities, more red flags appeared – the route he took to and from work each day passed directly along the Seattle strip where so many of the victims had been picked up; he had called in sick or on holiday for every one of the days on which a known victim had been murdered – and there was the 1980 arrest for allegedly choking a prostitute.

Finally, in 1987, investigators decided they had enough to execute a search warrant of his home. Detectives combed the house, taking away carpet fibres, ropes, anything they thought might match with evidence recovered from the victims, as well as hair and saliva samples from Ridgway himself.

Nothing matched, and once more, he walked.

Over the following decade, the teenage girls and young

women who had disappeared in 1982 and 1983 continued to be found with depressing regularity. By the turn of the millennium the bodies of all but five of the missing women had been recovered – 44 in total – but, after a series of false leads that saw the task force pursue avenues of investigation as far away as California, detectives were still no closer to finding their killer.

The Green River Killer remained at large. Although the murders seemed to have abated, he was nonetheless a constant threat and terror for the sex workers of Seattle, a lurking menace who might be behind the wheel of any of the vehicles cruising the strip.

In January 1998, Gary Ridgway struck for the final time. Aged 38, Patricia Yellowrobe was the oldest of his victims, but her chaotic lifestyle fitted his usual pattern. Alcoholic and homeless at the time of her death, she was found in bushes on waste ground south of Seattle seven months later. Despite the bruising to her face and neck, the coroner declared her death an accidental overdose, and her injuries little more than the sad consequence of her lifestyle.

Three years later, technology finally caught up with Ridgway. Although the trail had seemed irretrievably cold, in 2001 breakthroughs in DNA science meant that what remained of the task force was able to conduct more sophisticated analysis of samples taken from the victims decades before. When they ran semen recovered from the corpses of Marcia Chapman, Opal Mills and Cynthia Hinds through their databases, the three young women recovered from the Green River in August 1982 gave them a hit.

The saliva swab taken from Gary Ridgway in 1987 was a perfect match. On 30 November 2001, he was arrested at work. This time he would not walk free.

*

Initially charged with the murders of Chapman, Mills and Hinds, as well as of Carol Ann Christensen, whom he had killed in May 1983, the names of his first victim, Wendy Coffield, plus Debra Bonner and Debra Estes were added to Ridgway's indictment after further analysis matched microscopic paint particles on them to the brand Ridgway used at work at the time of their killings.

After two decades of dodging justice for his crimes, Ridgway knew the game was finally up. On 5 November 2003, he pleaded guilty to the murders of all 48 known victims of the Green River Killer – including that of Patricia Yellowrobe, whose cause of death had been revised after he confessed to killing her – as part of a plea deal that would spare him death row. In 2010 a forty-ninth life sentence was added, after a final, still-unidentified body was found.

Ridgway didn't stop there: he not only confessed to the known murders, but also claimed to have killed anything up to 41 other prostitutes, whose details he could not remember. His confession remains one of the most chillingly candid admissions of guilt in criminal history.

'I look like an ordinary person,' he said, describing how he would entice his victims into his truck. 'Here's a guy, he's not really muscle-bound . . . Just an ordinary john and that was their downfall. My appearance was different from what I really was.

'I would talk to her . . . and get her mind off of the . . . anything she was nervous about. And think, you know, she thinks, "Oh, this guy cares," . . . which I didn't. I just want to get her in the vehicle and eventually kill her.'

A forensic psychologist asked Ridgway to rate himself on a scale of one to five, with five being 'the worst kind of evil'. The man who was at that time America's most deadly serial killer gave himself a three.

'Why only three?' the psychologist asked.

'For one thing, is I killed 'em,' he replied. 'I didn't torture 'em. They went fast.'

12

TED BUNDY

(USA, 1974–8, 30–100 VICTIMS)

In the early hours of 1 February 1974, Lynda Ann Healy, a 21-year-old undergraduate at the University of Washington in Seattle, woke with a start. Somebody was in her basement apartment. She barely had time to register the shadowy figure by her bed before he swung something hard and heavy at her head, knocking her out cold.

The following day, when her parents arrived to take her to dinner, they found her sheets and pillowcase soaked in blood. There would be no trace of Lynda Ann until a year later, when part of her decapitated skull was found near Taylor Mountain, in the forests an hour's drive east of the city.

One month later, on 12 March, Donna Gail Manson, a

19-year-old student at nearby Evergreen State College, left her dormitory to attend a jazz concert. She was never seen again.

On 17 April, 18-year-old Susan Rancourt disappeared as she returned to her dormitory at Central Washington State College. There were no signs of struggle or indications of what might have happened to her until her skull was found 11 months later, buried near Lynda Ann Healy's at Taylor Mountain.

Three weeks after that, Roberta Parks, 22, was last seen leaving her room at Oregon State University, 260 miles south of Seattle, en route to a coffee date with friends. She disappeared in broad daylight; the remains of her jawbone were also found at Taylor Mountain the following March.

On 1 June, 22-year-old Brenda Carol Ball disappeared from the parking lot of a bar near Seattle-Tacoma Airport. Ten days later, 18-year-old University of Washington student Georgann Hawkins left her boyfriend's dormitory after midnight, heading for her sorority house. Somewhere along the short walk, she too vanished.

Six young women had disappeared in five months; all, with the exception of Lynda Ann Healy, vanished apparently into thin air, with no clues as to what might have happened to them. None were known to each other; all they had in common was the fact they were young, attractive, white college students, and, as one detective noted, all wore their long hair parted down the middle.

As panic spread among the university campuses, police desperately appealed for any information that might yield some kind of lead as to where the missing students might be or who might have taken them there, no matter how tenuous. Amid the flood of tips, a few stood out.

On the night of Susan Rancourt's disappearance – and also three evenings earlier – two Central Washington State students reported being approached by a handsome man wearing a sling on his arm, who asked for help carrying a pile of books to his brown Volkswagen Beetle. A man with a sling was also seen in the parking lot of the Flame Tavern near the airport at the time of Brenda Carol Ball's disappearance; and on 10 June 1974, just hours before Georgann Hawkins vanished, another female student reported being asked by a man with a leg cast and crutches to help carry his briefcase to his car – also a light-brown VW Beetle.

Beyond that, the police had nothing.

*

A decade before the Green River Killer terrorized the sex workers and runaways of Seattle and Tacoma, another menace stalked Washington State, raping and butchering young women and leaving no clues behind ... but there the similarities ended.

Where Gary Ridgway targeted the lost and abandoned Seattle underclass, this killer sought his victims from society's brightest, prettiest, most wholesome middle-class girls and young women. And where Ridgway was content to kill within a comfortable distance of his home, this killer went on to murder in at least five further states across the full length and breadth of America before being finally brought to justice.

He did not, to use Ridgway's phrase, 'kill 'em fast'. His victims were bludgeoned into unconsciousness, repeatedly raped and tortured, sometimes kept captive for days or even weeks, before being strangled. After their deaths they would often be decapitated and their heads kept as trophies. On at least one occasion, he incinerated a victim's skull in his fireplace before vacuuming up the ashes. Before his own execution he described himself as 'the most cold-hearted son of a bitch you'll ever meet'.

It remains unknown just how many young women Ted Bundy murdered – or even when he began killing. He confessed to 30 homicides, but few believe that to be the true tally: when FBI agents questioning him suggested he may have been responsible for 36 murders he replied, 'Add one digit to that and you'll have it.'

Did Ted Bundy kill 136 times? Did he kill 360 times? Or was he a fantasist as well as a maniac, and 'only' had 30 victims to his name? Whatever the truth, he remains one of the most fascinating, and horrifying, serial killers to have ever lived.

Over the course of his (known) five-year murder spree he grew in sophistication, meticulously planning his strikes and reconnoitring 'safe' sites from which to abduct his victims, before taking them to other pre-prepared locations to rape, torture, kill and dispose of them at his leisure. He left almost nothing in the way of physical or forensic evidence behind, and used his own knowledge of the law and policing to stay one step ahead of investigators.

He is also singular among serial killers for the intense

fascination he continues to hold over society nearly half a century after his capture. Before Ted Bundy (and to a great extent after him too), serial killers were characterized as outcasts, mentally and often physically impaired; they were shadowy bogeymen, psychotic freaks, Frankenstein's monsters. Bundy, on the other hand, was handsome, charming, intelligent, a university graduate and law student, a politically ambitious Republican Party go-getter, volunteer at Seattle's Suicide Hotline Crisis Center, assistant director of the Seattle Crime Prevention Advisory Commission and even worker at the Department of Emergency Services, a government agency involved in the search for the same missing women he had murdered.

He had the remarkable knack of being able to change his appearance seemingly at will. In photographs and mugshots he seems alternately good-looking and somehow forgettable, striking and bland, according to minor changes in hairstyle and attitude.

Bundy was not just the man next door – he was the man next door you aspired to be, or, more chillingly, the man next door you would be happy for your daughter to date. So much so that during the time he was killing and mutilating his dozens of victims, he maintained healthy romantic relationships with several women, one of whom he married even as he stood trial for murder.

In 1864, the French poet Charles Baudelaire wrote: 'The Devil's finest trick was to persuade the world he did not exist' – for Ted Bundy, that maxim was to be horribly prescient.

*

Theodore Robert Bundy was born on 24 November 1946. He never knew his father – it remains questionable just how well his mother, Eleanor Cowell, barely 18 at the time of his birth, did either. He was raised by his maternal grandparents in Philadelphia, with Eleanor posing as his older sister, before the family moved to Tacoma, Washington State, in 1950, where Eleanor married John Bundy. The couple had four children together, and John formally adopted Ted as his own son.

Accounts of Bundy's childhood depend on which of the versions he later told psychologists and detectives you choose to believe. He was either a loner, or a popular schoolboy, either a bully or chronically shy. What does seem indisputable, however, is that his teenage years saw a growing fascination with sex and violence. As a youth he would scour rubbish bins in search of magazines with pictures of naked women or crime novels that depicted sexual violence. He became a peeping Tom, waiting in the shadows to catch a glimpse of his neighbours undressing through open windows.

According to one Tacoma resident, the young Bundy also developed a sadistic streak, catching stray cats, dousing them in lighter fluid and setting light to them, as well as taking younger children into the woods to torment. 'He'd strip them down, take their clothes,' childhood neighbour Sandi Holt told TV reporters in 2019. 'You'd hear them screaming for blocks.'

When Bundy was 14, one such younger child disappeared from her home close to his household. Anne Marie Burr was eight years old and lived on Ted's newspaper round route; she vanished on 31 August 1961 and her body has never been found. In typically cryptic style, Bundy himself has simultaneously denied having anything to do with her disappearance, while also claiming he had 'stalked, strangled and sexually mauled [his] first victim, an eight-year-old girl'.

After graduating from high school, Bundy enrolled at the University of Washington to study Chinese, where he also volunteered for the Republican Party, before winning a scholarship to Stanford University, re-enrolling at Washington as a psychology major (graduating in 1972), and eventually matriculating at Seattle University School of Law.

Allied to this stellar academic career was a healthy love life: as well as dating several different women through his twenties, Bundy fostered a number of serious romantic relationships. One was with Diane Edwards, a fellow University of Washington graduate known for wearing her long hair parted down the middle. He later described Edwards as 'the only woman I ever really loved' – but abruptly ended their relationship in January 1974, even as the couple discussed marriage.

Within a few weeks of the split, students in Washington and Oregon began disappearing.

On 14 July, five weeks after killing Georgann Hawkins, Bundy struck again. Four separate female witnesses described being approached by a man in tennis whites at Lake Sammamish State Park, a popular water-sports and boating resort to the east of Seattle. His arm was in a sling, and introducing himself as 'Ted', he asked each of them for help in unloading his sailboat from the back of his VW Beetle. Three of the young women refused, the fourth ran away when she saw there was no boat.

Janice Ann Ott, 23, did not refuse, or flee, but instead accompanied Bundy to his car. He knocked her out, bundled her into the passenger seat, and drove two miles east into the woods to an isolated logging road, where he tied, bound, gagged and brutally raped her.

Four hours later, he returned to the lake and repeated the sailboat trick, this time luring Denise Marie Naslund, a 19-year-old computer studies student, into his car before bludgeoning her unconscious.

When Denise came to, she was lying next to the still-alive Janice Ott. Satisfied both were conscious, Bundy forced one to watch as he strangled the other. After they were dead he once again had sex with the corpses, before decapitating and burying them.

In September their remains would be found, along with an additional thigh bone and vertebrae belonging to a third young woman, whom Bundy later identified as Georgann Hawkins. Six months later, the skulls and jawbone fragments of Lynda Ann Healy, Susan Rancourt, Roberta Parks and Brenda Carol Ball were unearthed at Taylor Mountain, just a few miles further into the forest.

Donna Gail Manson, the 19-year-old Evergreen student who had disappeared on her way to a jazz concert in March, has never been found. Her skull is thought to have been among those that Bundy burned and then hoovered up.

The abduction and murders of Janice Ann Ott and Denise Naslund had been Bundy's most audacious to date – but in his eagerness to find a target he had given police a valuable lead. A description of the suspect with the sling and fake sailboat was made public, along with the fact he drove a Beetle and went by the name of 'Ted'.

Once again, the tip hotline lit up. Among the hundreds of calls were two workers at the Department of Emergency Services and a University of Washington professor who voiced their concerns that the description matched a VW-driving Seattle student by the name of Ted Bundy.

Police looked into it – and then dismissed the idea. Bundy was a clean-cut, handsome man in a steady relationship – and a law student and psychology graduate too. He worked for the Republican Party and local government agencies and volunteered at a suicide crisis centre ... hardly the profile of a monstrous serial killer.

Ted Bundy was ruled out as a suspect, and the investigation remained open.

*

In August 1974, Bundy moved to Salt Lake City, after accepting a place at the University of Utah Law School. As the spate of murders around Seattle abruptly stopped, a new series of killings began 1,000 miles to the south-east.

The first victim of his 'second phase' remains unidentified to this day. According to his eventual confession, Bundy picked up and strangled a hitchhiker on 2 September in Idaho, north of Utah, before photographing her dismembered corpse and throwing it into a river. Exactly one month later he snatched 16-year-old Nancy Wilcox as she walked on a road in a suburb of Salt Lake City. After beating and restraining her, he drove her back to his apartment, where for 24 hours she was subjected to prolonged, repeated and sadistic torture and sexual assault, before finally being strangled. Whatever remained of her afterwards has never been found.

Nancy Wilcox had awakened a new depravity in Bundy: he kept his next victim, 17-year-old Melissa Anne Smith, who was the daughter of a Salt Lake City chief of police, alive and in agony in his apartment for a full week after her abduction on 18 October. Her battered, naked body was found in the mountains on 27 October, her skull partially caved in by a crowbar.

On 28 November, another body was found. Seventeen-year-old Laura Ann Aime had last been seen leaving a Halloween party on 31 October; her post-mortem indicated she had been kept alive for up to 20 days after her disappearance. Both she and Smith had been repeatedly raped, sodomized and eventually garrotted with nylon stockings.

By the time Aime's corpse was discovered Bundy had struck for a thirteenth confirmed time. On 8 November, after unsuccessfully attempting to abduct 18-year-old Carol DaRonch in a southern suburb of Salt Lake City – she managed to jump from his car as he tried to handcuff her – he snatched 17-year-old Debra Kent following a theatre production at her school and took her back to his apartment, where she remained for a full day and night before he disposed of her body. When later asked how long he had kept her alive before murdering her, Bundy replied: 'Let's see, during half of it.' All that has ever been recovered of her is a single kneecap bone.

After Christmas, Bundy shifted his attention eastwards.

On 12 January, nurse Caryn Campbell, 23, disappeared from her holiday apartment in Snowmass Village, Colorado, around 400 miles from Salt Lake City. Her naked body was discovered 36 days later – she had been killed by repeated blows to the head, and her body was scored by dozens of deep cuts.

On 15 March Bundy returned to his favourite means of enticing a victim into his car: ski instructor Julie Cunningham, 26, was approached by a handsome man on crutches in the resort of Vail, Colorado. Taking pity on him, she was only too happy to help carry his ski boots – once they reached the VW Beetle, he clubbed her into unconsciousness, before handcuffing her, driving her into the Colorado wilderness and raping, beating and finally strangling her. Three weeks later, 25-year-old Denise Oliverson disappeared near the Utah–Colorado border: neither her nor Cunningham's bodies have ever been found.

The following month Bundy snatched 12-year-old Lynette Culver from the street by her school in Pocatello, Idaho, 170 miles north of Salt Lake City, took her to a hotel room and raped her before drowning her in the bath and throwing her body into the Snake River; and on 28 June, Susan Curtis, a 15-year-old schoolgirl attending a youth conference in Salt Lake City, became his eighteenth named victim. As with so many of those he killed, the whereabouts of her remains are still unknown.

For 18 months, Ted Bundy had terrorized girls and young women across five states in two frantic killing campaigns that had seen him murder at a rate of at least once a month. Now, finally, investigators were about to catch up with him.

*

Back in Washington, detectives had made use of what was then cutting-edge database technology to narrow down their suspects: after cross-checking everything that was known about the suspected killer – including men in their late twenties and early thirties called Ted, VW Beetle owners, those familiar with university campuses, and so on – one name kept recurring: Theodore Bundy.

And then on 16 August 1975, he fell into their lap. A highway patrol officer pulled Bundy's Beetle over after watching him cruising the Salt Lake City suburbs in the early morning; the resulting search of his car turned up a ski mask, crowbar, pantyhose, rope, handcuffs and an ice pick. Although this was suspicious, it wasn't enough to hold Bundy, but after releasing him, Salt Lake City police placed him under 24-hour surveillance.

Bundy was on their radar, and he knew it – but he also believed himself too clever for the police, later scoffing that during the search detectives had missed a stack of polaroid photographs of the dead women that would have seen him immediately jailed.

He wasn't quite clever enough. Weeks later, Bundy sold his Beetle: the police immediately impounded it, and after a forensic examination uncovered hair strands matching Caryn Campbell and Melissa Smith, he was put in a line-up and identified by Carol DaRonch as the man who had tried to force her into his car the previous November. In October he was arrested on aggravated kidnapping charges, and in June 1976 sentenced to 15 years in prison. The murder of Caryn Campbell was added to his indictment a few months later and in January 1977 he was transferred to Aspen, Colorado, to stand trial.

But Ted Bundy wasn't done yet. In June, during a preliminary hearing, he escaped from the courthouse through an open window and went on the run for six days in the mountains before being caught.

Transferred once again, this time to Colorado Springs jail, Bundy lasted just six more months behind bars before once again breaking out.

Using the same charisma that had enticed so many young women to their deaths, he persuaded fellow inmates, as well as long-standing girlfriend Carol Boone, whom he had been dating since the time of his first murder spree and who was convinced of his innocence, to supply him with a floor plan of the jail, as well as a hacksaw blade and $500 in cash.

On 30 December 1977, with the jail manned by skeleton staff for the Christmas break, he sawed through the steel bars on the ceiling of his cell, hoisted himself into the crawl space, wriggled through to the chief jailer's quarters, changed clothes and strolled out of the prison to freedom. By the time anyone even noticed he was gone, he was headed for Florida.

If Ted Bundy viewed his escape from prison as a chance to reinvent himself and drop off the police radar for good, either the thought was soon dismissed, or else his murderous urges were by this time too all-consuming to resist. Sixteen hundred miles from Colorado Springs, he managed just two weeks before killing again.

Shortly before 3am on 15 January 1978, he broke into a sorority house on the Florida State University campus and attacked no fewer than four students in a devastating psychotic rampage. Margaret Bowman, 21, and 20-year-old Lisa Levy were bludgeoned with a piece of wood as they slept, then sexually assaulted, and garrotted to death with a nylon stocking. Levy was also bitten so hard in the attack that one of her nipples was nearly torn off.

Even as they lay dying he had already moved into another room, where he set about battering roommates Kathy Kleiner and Karen Chandler, both 21, breaking both their jaws and smashing Kleiner's teeth – they were only saved from their friends' fates after a sudden light outside the dormitory spooked him.

Bundy was off campus before any serious alarm could be raised. From the time he entered the girls' building to the moment he fled again, his furious attack on the four students had lasted just 15 minutes.

And still he wasn't done. After leaving the sorority house he broke into a student apartment just a few blocks away and clubbed 21-year-old student Cheryl Thomas as she slept, fracturing her skull in five places, before sexually assaulting her. She was saved by her neighbours, who, alarmed by the sudden noise, called the police. By the time they arrived to find Thomas lying in a pool of her own blood on the bed, Bundy had once again disappeared.

He was to kill one final time before the nightmare was over.

On 8 February, he stole a car and drove 100 miles east, to the sleepy town of Lake City. The following morning, 12-year-old Kimberly Diane Leach disappeared from Lake City Junior High School, running an errand between classes. When her remains were found in a nearby Florida State Park seven weeks later, she had been beaten and raped, and had bled to death from severe lacerations to her throat.

One week later a traffic cop pulled Bundy over in the Florida city of Pensacola, on suspicion of driving a stolen car. He tried to run but was overpowered; as the officer cuffed him he told him: 'I wish you had killed me.'

*

Ted Bundy stood trial for the Florida State University killings and assaults in June 1979 – such was his notoriety that it was covered by over 200 reporters and became the first trial to be televised nationally. Despite his playing up to the cameras, deploying all his charisma, charm and good looks and even representing himself in his own defence, it took a jury just seven hours to convict him, and on 24 July he was sentenced to death.

Six months later he was back in the dock for the murder of schoolgirl Kimberly Leach – and once again he played the showman, proposing marriage to long-term girlfriend Carol Boone in the courthouse. Much to the delight of the hundreds of reporters, she accepted. On 10 February 1980, he was found guilty and given a third death sentence.

Ted Bundy was only ever convicted of the murders of three people, but during his time on death row he engaged in a series of extraordinary confessions with reporters and investigators in which he calmly and matter-of-factly described how he had slaughtered at least 27 other girls and young women, as well as his habit of revisiting their graves after their deaths to have sex with the corpses. He also explained that after decapitating his victims he kept several of their heads in his apartment as trophies, before finally disposing of them. 'The big payoff for me,' he said, 'was actually possessing whatever it was I had stolen ... The ultimate possession was, in fact, the taking of the life.'

On the morning of 24 January 1989, Ted Bundy was executed by electric chair. The handsome, charismatic devil who managed to persuade the world he didn't exist had finally been unmasked; he left behind a terrible legacy, the extent of which remains unknown to this day. As the execution was carried out, hundreds celebrated outside the prison.

13

STEVEN WRIGHT

(UK, 2006, 5+ VICTIMS)

November is a miserable month for those selling sex on British city streets. The nights grow ever longer, the autumn rains turn icier, the wind more bitter, more biting. The short skirts necessary to attract business offer no protection against the elements; skin exposed for hours in the cold numbs and turns blue. And with the worsening weather comes an attendant drop in trade – the casual and the curious, the nervous first-timers who might chance a punt in the warmer months, won't venture out in bad weather; and all you're left with are your regulars, if you're lucky enough to have them, or else the hardened users, for whom a prostitute is barely a person at all.

There is also a third category: the crazies. When the nights are darker and the weather nastier, the street girls keep an even closer eye than usual on their trade. The choice between freezing on kerbsides for ever-longer hours to scrape a few pounds together, and the dangers of whose car you might be getting into, can mean running a nightly, even hourly, risk of rape, assault, or worse.

In the final few months of 2006, sex workers on the drab and drizzly streets of Ipswich's red light district in Suffolk, eastern England, faced exactly this choice. For some of them, it would prove fatal.

*

Some serial killers like to boast, once they are caught, about how and why they committed their crimes; others see a confession as a kind of unburdening, laying out, in sometimes sickening detail, every last aspect and facet of the murders in the hope of a sort of absolution. Some are matter-of-fact about their reasons for killing, others attempt to justify their compulsions – either through Ian Brady-style quasi-philosophy, or else by invoking childhood traumas and psychological issues of their own. Some are certifiably insane, their motives impossible to ever unravel – and still others don't talk at all.

In the space of 42 terrifying days between 30 October and 10 December 2006, Steven Wright, a 48-year-old former pub landlord, cruise-ship steward and forklift truck driver, killed at least five prostitutes he picked up from the streets near his house in Ipswich.

He has never given a detailed confession to the murders, nor has he ever shown remorse for his victims. Neither detectives nor the families of those he murdered have any clue as to why he killed them; it is highly unlikely they ever will.

The women Wright murdered were all aged between 19 and 29, and although they came from a variety of different backgrounds, had all developed crippling drug addictions at an early age, which led them into prostitution as a means of paying for their habit.

Wright was well known to all of them, as a long-standing and habitual customer of prostitutes; at his trial he admitted to paying for sex from four of them. And yet, although all of his victims were naked when their bodies were found, there was no evidence of sexual assault. Two had been asphyxiated, but no conclusive cause of death could be established for the other three. Two of the corpses had been arranged in a cruciform pose post-mortem.

Why did Wright target the same sex workers he patronized? Why did he strip them naked but leave their bodies unmolested? Why did he arrange two as if crucified? And if only two were strangled, how did he kill the other three?

In a case of so many unanswered 'whys'?, one question stands out above all: just what could tip a man with no previous recorded history of criminal violence into such a vicious and prolific killing binge at the age of 48?

*

Steven Wright's early life was unremarkable, if not especially happy. He was born in April 1958, in Ipswich's neighbouring county of Norfolk, the second of four children to a military policeman father and veterinary nurse mother; his parents divorced and both remarried when he was young, and he was raised by his father.

After leaving school aged 16, he joined the merchant navy and found work as a chef on cross-Channel ferries and then as a steward on the cruise ship *Queen Elizabeth 2*. He married and divorced twice before he was 30, and after leaving the navy was employed in a series of low-level industries, labouring on the docks and working as a lorry driver and a forklift truck operator, as well as managing pubs in Norwich and London.

But throughout his twenties and thirties, as he struggled between monotonous jobs and failing relationships, an anger was building inside Wright.

His time in charge of the first pub he managed, the Ferry Boat Inn, situated at the heart of Norwich's red light district, was a disappointment: the pub was a regular hangout for the city's prostitutes and their pimps, and keeping control of the often-tricky clientele proved too much for him to handle. He lasted just five months before quitting and taking a job as a barman in the London suburb of Bromley, before trying again, as manager of the Rose and Crown in Plumstead, east London.

If the Ferry Boat Inn hadn't worked out, the Rose and Crown was a disaster. His stints behind the bar had made him a heavy drinker; now, as the business struggled, he directed his growing unhappiness into gambling – and by 1993, just three years after taking the position at the Rose and Crown, his increasingly erratic behaviour proved too much for the pub's owners, and he was fired.

Drinking and gambling were not Wright's only vices. Already familiar with sex workers after first visiting prostitutes during shore leave abroad with the QE2, he had become a regular patron of massage parlours and brothels in south and east London. Between the booze and the gambling and the sex, he began to rack up huge debts.

In 1994, he finally cracked. Jobless, twice divorced, and bankrupt, he attempted to gas himself in his car. A passer-by found him lying unconscious in an alley in the village of Haverhill in Suffolk; he was rushed to hospital and survived unscathed.

In 2000 he tried again, overdosing on pills after returning from a sex tourism trip to Thailand that he had financed by once again accruing huge debts. That attempt too, like so much else in his life to date, ended a failure.

The following year his debts also led to his only other brush with the law. After being caught stealing £80 from a pub till, he was convicted of theft, and according to standard procedure, his DNA added to the national criminal database.

If two unsuccessful suicide attempts and a criminal conviction within seven years were to mark rock bottom for Wright, just a few months after his arrest he was to meet the woman who it seemed would give him a chance to finally turn things around and make something positive of his life.

In 2001, while living back with his father in Felixstowe, just 10 miles from Ipswich, he met Pamela Wright (their surnames were a coincidence). Eleven years older than him, she was a calmer, steadier influence than either of his previous wives; the two of them started dating, and three years later they moved into a house together in Ipswich. Wright kicked his gambling habit, cut down on his drinking, and for a little while at least, stopped visiting massage parlours.

It wasn't to last. While he worked as a forklift driver during the day, Pamela took a position on the night shift at an IT call centre. They barely saw each other, and after he dropped her at work each evening, he once again began visiting Ipswich's massage parlours.

Within a year the habit was once again proving too expensive, and Wright looked for cheaper ways to get his kicks. He soon discovered he could haggle a price for sex with the girls working the street corners – and the more desperate and drug-addicted they were, the cheaper a price he could barter them down to.

By the autumn of 2006 Wright had become a well-known figure among Ipswich's sex workers. If he wasn't exactly well liked – his insistence on securing the girls' services for as little money as he could get away with saw to that – he wasn't hated either. He certainly wasn't classed as a 'crazy'. They even had nicknames for him: the 'Silver Backed Gorilla', and 'Mondeo Man', in reference to the car he drove to cruise the streets.

But at the end of October, something happened to change Wright's attitude to the prostitutes he had become so familiar with. And to this day, nobody has any idea what it was.

*

On 30 October 2006, Tania Nicol, a 19-year-old Ipswich local all her life, left her mother's house and headed towards her regular strip on Handford Road, towards the western edge of the city, where the tired terraces peter out into industrial and commercial estates. Her addiction to heroin and cocaine had forced her to sell her body, first in the more protected massage parlours, and then, as her habit grew worse, on the streets.

When she didn't come home, her mother called the police, and a week later, with still no word, issued a public appeal for information. There would be no clue as to Tania's whereabouts until 8 December, when her naked body was found floating in a river near Copdock Mill, just outside Ipswich.

A week after she disappeared, another working girl went missing. Gemma Adams, 25, had been raised in a comfortable middle-class family in the Suffolk village of Kesgrave, but, like Nicol, had fallen under the spell of heroin as a teenager. It had cost her her job at an insurance agency, after which she drifted into prostitution to fund her habit. By November 2006 she was living with her boyfriend in Ipswich's red light district – he too was a heroin addict, and knew of her sex work.

On 14 November, she left the house they shared and made her way to West End Road in search of punters: she was last seen at 1.15 the following morning, outside a BMW dealership.

Three weeks later, on 2 December, Gemma became the first of Wright's victims to be found. It is not known how or why he killed her – when her naked body was discovered lying in a stream near the village of Hintlesham, a few miles west of the city, there were no signs of sexual assault, and although she had certainly been murdered, a definite cause of death could not be established. When her parents were told of her death, they had no idea she was working as a prostitute.

Over the next three days another two sex workers disappeared.

Anneli Alderton, a 24-year-old mother of one, had gone off the rails following the death of her father when she was just 16. After running away from home she had become addicted to heroin and crack cocaine and spent four spells in prison for theft. By December 2006 she was living in Colchester in Essex, but for the past few weeks had been catching the train to work the streets of Ipswich, where she had struck up friendships with Gemma Adams and Tania Nicol. Less than 24 hours after Adams's corpse was discovered, she too vanished from the Handford Road area.

Two days later, 29-year-old Annette Nicholls, a former beautician whose addiction to heroin had also driven her into sex work, was reported missing by her mother, frightened by the news of the three other sex workers' sudden disappearances. Unlike the other victims, Annette was last seen in the east of the city, close to the town centre. Like the others, there seemed to be no clue as to what had happened to her.

By the end of the first week of December 2006, four young women had disappeared from the streets of Ipswich's red light district in a little over a month, but so far only one body had turned up. Although concern was growing among those close to the missing women, the chaotic nature of their lifestyles and their serious drug addictions meant that police remained wary of jumping to any sinister conclusions regarding possible links to the murder of Gemma Adams.

Over the course of four horrifying days, that was all to change.

On 8 December, Tania Nicol was found, floating near Copdock Mill. As with Gemma Adams, she too had been stripped of all her clothes, and like Adams again, there were no signs of sexual assault, and no clear cause of death could be determined. The similarities were too obvious to be ignored, and, although the police were still keen not to overly frighten the public, privately a suspicion grew that a serial killer was at large in the city.

On 10 December, another Ipswich sex worker disappeared. Paula Clennell, 24, had been born in Northumberland but moved to Ipswich after the break-up of her parents' marriage. She had become addicted to drugs as a teenager, and after her three children were taken from her by social services, her addiction became crippling. Desperate, she turned to prostitution, and just a few days before her disappearance she had spoken to a local news crew about her intention to keep working, despite the deaths of Tania Nicol and Gemma Adams, explaining simply: 'I need the money.'

The same day Paula went missing, the lifeless body of Anneli Alderton was found by a member of the public in woods near the village of Nacton, five miles south-east of Ipswich city centre. She too was naked and unmolested, though curiously her limbs had been arranged in a cruciform pose. Her post-mortem revealed that she had been asphyxiated, and that she was three months pregnant when she was killed.

The peculiar positioning of her corpse puzzled police – was this a different killer from that of Adams and Nicol? Or was it simply an attempt by the murderer to put detectives off the scent? They concluded it was the latter, and in a televised press conference admitted for the first time that they might be looking for a serial killer.

'There are some distinct similarities [between the deaths of Alderton, Adams and Nicol],' said Detective Chief Superintendent Stewart Gull. 'We have already linked the deaths of Tania and Gemma; clearly there are significant similarities in the finding of this latest woman.'

The police also issued a plea to the sex workers of Ipswich to keep away from the red light area. 'My message to you is simple,' said Assistant Chief Constable Jacqui Cheer. 'Stay off the streets. If you are out alone at night you are putting yourself in danger.'

The very next day, another press conference was hurriedly called. Annette Nicholls and Paula Clennell had both been found close to each other a short way outside Ipswich, near Nacton. Both were naked, both had not been sexually assaulted, and both showed signs of having been strangled to death. Annette had been placed in the same cruciform position as Anneli Alderton; Paula's corpse appeared to have been hurriedly dumped a short way off the road.

Five bodies had been found in 11 days; there was now no

doubt that a serial killer was stalking the streets of Ipswich. Once again, police urged sex workers not to go out at night, and they launched a huge murder investigation.

Over the following days, more than 650 police officers took part in 'Operation Sumac', with a tip line set up receiving more than 10,000 calls. Within a week, they got their man.

*

In the end, what caught Steven Wright was the £80 he stole from a till shortly after his second suicide attempt in 2001. Samples of DNA found on the victims were run through the national criminal database, and after they matched the swabs he gave following his theft conviction, he was arrested. Further forensic searches of his clothes, car and home revealed more evidence linking him to each of the five dead women, including blood spots on the outside of his jacket and in his car.

His defence, that he had paid each of them for sex but nothing more, did not wash with the jury. On 21 February 2008, he was found guilty on all five counts of murder and sentenced to life imprisonment with the recommendation of no chance of parole.

In his summing up, the judge had a strong message for the jury.

'The loss of these young lives is a tragedy,' he said. 'You may view with some distaste the lifestyles of those involved [but] whatever the drugs they took, whatever the work they did, no one is entitled to do these women any harm, let alone kill them.'

And still, Steven Wright refused to explain why he did it, or what drove him to suddenly and dramatically change from user of prostitutes to serial prostitute killer. The general conclusion among investigators, journalists and psychologists was simply that decades of frustration and failure had fostered a slowly growing anger that suddenly boiled over into 42 days of madness and violence.

Was that really the explanation – or was something else entirely going on?

After his conviction, detectives admitted that Wright was now under investigation in connection with other unsolved murders – most notably a cluster of sex worker killings in Norwich in the 1990s and early 2000s. Psychologists have stated that it is 'highly unusual' for serial killers to begin murdering at the age of 48 and several criminologists involved in the investigation into Wright's Ipswich murders have said that the killings did not bear the hallmarks of a first-time murderer, but rather of someone who had struck before.

The investigations into Steven Wright continue.

14

ROBERT HANSEN

(USA, 1971–83, 17+ VICTIMS)

On 13 June 1983, officers at Anchorage Police Department, Alaska, took an unusual call. A truck driver had phoned in to say he had picked up a teenage girl hitchhiking near Merrill Field Airport. She was terrified, dishevelled, bruised, her hands were cuffed and she was barefoot, and she was screaming something about a man who wanted to fly her out to his cabin in the Alaskan wilderness and kill her.

The trucker had left her at a motel; when police officers arrived to question the girl she was still handcuffed, still barefoot, and she told them a story that made their blood run cold.

Earlier that day she had been touting for business outside a strip bar, when a man had offered her $200 to perform oral sex on him. He was kind of a geeky-looking guy, she told police, skinny, clean-shaven, with glasses and a stutter – definitely not the kind of brawny, macho Alaskan men who made up her usual client base – and she barely gave it a second thought before getting in his car.

The second the passenger door shut, everything changed. The man pulled a gun and told her he had changed his mind. Now they were going to his home, and he had different plans for her.

Once inside his house he took her into the basement where he handcuffed her, chained her by the neck to a post, stripped her naked and spent the next few hours repeatedly and violently raping her. When he had tired of that, he calmly told her to put her clothes back on: he had changed his mind again, they were now going to fly out in his plane to his hunting cabin in the wilderness north-east of the city.

He did not explain what it was he intended to do with her once they got there, but after the violence he had already shown, she could make a pretty good guess.

At Merrill Field Airport, she grabbed her chance to escape. As the man turned his back to load up his single-engine plane, she made a run for it, diving out of the car still handcuffed and racing towards the busy Sixth Avenue freeway that ran alongside the airfield.

Before she fled she kicked off her shoes and pushed them under the passenger seat. Her name was Cindy Paulson, she was just 17 years old, and she was the key to capturing one of America's most nightmarish killers.

*

Alaska is America's largest and wildest state – twice the size of Texas and covering an area greater than France, Germany and Britain combined, it nevertheless has a tiny population roughly the same size as that of Seattle. Almost all of these inhabitants live in the cities of Juneau, Fairbanks and Anchorage – the rest of the 663,000 square miles is a vast, beautiful and spectacular terrain of mountains, forests, and unspoilt, largely uncharted, wilderness.

It's easy to disappear in the Alaskan wild, if you're not careful. And it's easy to make people disappear, too.

Over 12 years between 1971 and 1983, dozens of young women went missing from the streets of Anchorage. Twelve of their bodies would be found in the dense forests, dark gravel pits and freezing lakes around the Knik River and Matanuska-Susitna Valley, hundreds of miles from the city, many of them in areas only accessible by plane or boat. Most were prostitutes or topless dancers in the city's notoriously rough-and-ready red light district. Some had been shot; the remains of others were too badly mauled and eaten by wild animals to determine a cause of death.

The man who killed them was an awkward, married father-of-two who ran a popular bakery in Anchorage and talked with a pronounced stutter. He had moved to the city with his family in 1967 and, like many Alaskans, had a passion for hunting, winning prizes in 1969, 1970 and 1971 for the animals he killed in the mountains.

It was not until his eventual arrest that anyone but his victims knew of the terror that lay behind his quiet, affable exterior – or that his real passion was for hunting not wild animals, but human prey.

*

Robert Christian Hansen was born in February 1939 in rural Iowa to a Danish immigrant baker and his American wife. He was a skinny, awkward child, forced to work long hours in the bakery by his strict father, and despite being left-handed, made to write with his right hand; the resulting stress gave him a severe stutter, which would last the rest of his life.

The only escape from his lonely, mostly friendless childhood was hunting: encouraged by his father, he became a skilled archer and a crack shot with the rifle, spending hours in the woods near his home, stalking wild turkey, rabbits, and later whitetail and mule deer.

After leaving school, he took his passion into the United States Army Reserve and, after a year, to the police academy in the Iowan city of Pocahontas where he became an assistant drill instructor. It was while working there that he married his first wife, when he was aged 21.

The marriage was to last barely six months, a casualty of what, with the benefit of hindsight, would be the first manifestation of Hansen's psychopathic tendencies.

In December 1960, he persuaded a 16-year-old employee at his father's bakery to help him burn down the bus garage of his former school. Hansen had spent the three years since graduating nursing a simmering resentment for the unpopularity and loneliness he had felt while a student there – the arson was an act of revenge against both the institution itself, and also, symbolically, against his former classmates and teachers.

The 16-year-old turned him in, and Hansen was sentenced to three years in prison, where he was diagnosed with manic depression, as well as an 'infantile personality' with a tendency to obsess over anyone he felt had insulted or wronged him. He served 20 months, and his wife divorced him while he was incarcerated.

Three years later he married again, and in 1967 he moved with his new family to Anchorage, where he opened his own bakery, and quickly became a well-liked member of the community, joining a hunting lodge and becoming a father to two children.

He also invested in a cabin in the forests near the Knik River and bought a Piper PA-18 Super Cub two-seat, single-engine monoplane, which he kept at Merrill Field airstrip. At weekends he would fly north, landing on one of the many gravel bars along the river, and spend a few days at his cabin, hunting in the wild with not another human soul for miles around.

Hansen may have established a new life in America's most remote state, but he had also brought his psychological demons with him. Within four years he would once again face serious criminal charges – for the attempted rape of an unidentified woman and the rape of a prostitute. His lawyers plea-bargained the charges down to assault with a deadly weapon, and after serving just six months of his five-year sentence, he was once again a free man.

It is now believed that the two women who brought charges against Hansen in 1971 were not the first he had raped. And by then he had already started killing.

*

Anchorage may be the biggest conurbation in Alaska, but by most standards it is a small city. In 1971 it had a population of just 49,000. Home to adventurers, hunters, and blue-collar workers in the oil and gas industries, it also has one of the highest crime rates of any US city – with incidents of violent crime four times the national average.

Much of the trouble at that time was centred on the 'Tenderloin' district, an area around Fourth Avenue in the north of the city packed with nightclubs and strip joints, peep shows and shops selling pornography. Many of the women who worked as dancers in the clubs also hustled as prostitutes on the side, or else made extra cash posing for nude pictures sold at pop-up magazine stalls on the sidewalks. In the 1970s and '80s, Anchorage's Tenderloin district still had a lawless, frontier-town atmosphere – in such a remote state, separated from the rest of the Union, there was a feeling that, for some at least, anything goes.

It was in these topless bars and go-go clubs that Robert Hansen trawled for his victims. For a few hundred dollars he could persuade one of the dancers to leave with him; more often than not the money would not be paid and the services still taken. While it took until 1971 before anyone formally accused him of sexual assault, police now believe that Hansen had been preying on the sex workers for years before that.

By the end of 1971, rape was no longer enough for him; and he took his abuses of the women he picked up to a terrifying new level.

On the evening of 22 December 1971, 18-year-old Celia van Zanten disappeared in Anchorage as she walked to a supermarket. Three days later, her body was found in Chugach State Park, a vast expanse of mountains and forests to the east of the city. She had been brutally raped, her chest was sliced open with a knife, and her hands had been bound. It was not the knife wound that killed Celia – her autopsy revealed that she had died from exposure after being thrown, still alive, into a ravine. Abrasions on her hands and arms showed that in her last hours she had made a desperate, futile attempt to climb back out of the canyon.

Over the following years, more young women disappeared from Anchorage, but no further bodies surfaced for nine years.

Twenty-four-year-old Joanne Messina worked as a topless dancer in the Tenderloin, and on 19 May 1980 had accepted an invitation to dinner with Hansen. After their meal, he attempted to kiss her; she told him if he wanted anything more, he would have to pay for it like everyone else. Sure, he said, but after they reached his house, he told her they would play a different game instead.

Binding and gagging her, he bundled her into the back of his truck and drove south-east, deep into the forests – and with what would be an example of his chilling clarity of thought, brought her dog too. Once in the wild he shot the dog, later explaining that he did not want the animal leading the authorities to her grave.

Messina was struck on the head with his revolver, and then set free. For a moment she froze, still dizzy from the blow, unable to believe he was actually letting her go . . . before her survival instinct kicked in and she ran for all she was worth.

Hansen watched her scramble away and then, ever the expert hunter, picked up his rifle, took careful aim at the receding figure and killed her with two pinpoint accurate shots in the back. Her body was dumped into a gravel pit, the dog thrown into the river, and he calmly drove back to Anchorage. When she was discovered two months later, her corpse had been half-eaten by wolves.

Two weeks afterwards another body was found in the woods by the village of Eklutna, north of Anchorage. Also horribly decomposed and ravaged by wild animals, she had been stabbed in the back, but little else could be determined concerning who she was or how she had met her fate. The police dubbed her 'Eklutna Annie', and Hansen later said she was a prostitute and topless dancer. She has still never been properly identified.

The killings of Eklutna Annie and Joanne Messina were to prove typical of what became Robert Hansen's deadly modus operandi. Sex workers or exotic dancers were picked up in the Tenderloin – some, like Cindy Paulson, straight-up approached for sex, others either asked out for dinner, or else promised a few hundred dollars to pose for photographs. None of the women suspected the self-conscious-looking man with glasses and a stutter to be anything other than he appeared; but after getting into his car, all were cuffed, bound and kidnapped.

Some would first be driven to his cellar to be raped and tortured, others were taken straight out into the Alaskan wild, either by car or in his plane. Once in the forest, the lucky ones would die quickly. The others would be stripped naked, their ankles unbound and told to run for their lives.

Hansen would give them a head start – sometimes, if he was feeling particularly confident, of an hour or two – before following their trail, armed with a hunting knife and a .223 calibre rifle. When he caught up with them – and he always did – he would shoot them like he used to shoot wild turkey as a kid in Iowa. Some of their bodies were thrown into the river, others buried in gravel pits or shallow graves. The rest were left for the wolves.

Between the discovery of Celia van Zanten in 1971 and the last-ditch escape of Cindy Paulson from Merrill Field airstrip in June 1983, Hansen killed at least 17 young women in this manner, hunting them down like animals in remote spots across hundreds of miles of Alaskan wilderness around Anchorage, though mostly near his cabin by the Knik River in the Matanuska-Susitna Valley.

*

Anchorage police had been suspicious that a serial killer was operating in the city since September 1982, when the body of a third woman was found on the banks of the Knik River. Sherry Morrow, a 23-year-old stripper, had vanished the previous November, after telling friends she had an appointment with a photographer who was going to pay her $300 to pose for nude images. When her remains were found, she had been shot three times in the back with a .223 hunting rifle; forensic examination also revealed that she had been naked when killed, and then her clothes put back on after her death.

Following her discovery, the local authorities requested the help of the FBI to build up a profile of the man they believed to be behind the murders of all three bodies. The resulting report stated that the killer was probably suffering from low self-esteem, would keep souvenirs akin to hunting trophies of those he killed, and most remarkably, that he might speak with an impediment, such as a stutter.

After Cindy Paulson told police of her rape and assault at Hansen's home – and her frantic escape from the runway at Merrill Field – Hansen was duly brought in. Astonishingly, the police not only believed his denials, backed up by a false alibi he had secured from a friend, but even when confronted by Paulson's sneakers in his car, chose to take the word of the respectable local baker over the teenage prostitute. Hansen walked free . . . but not for long.

Detectives from the task force investigating the missing dancers and sex workers of the Tenderloin, many of whom had last been seen, like Sherry Morrow, after telling friends that they were going to meet a man who had promised to pay them in exchange for their time or for a nude photo shoot, took another look at the FBI profile of their suspect. The similarities with Hansen were too obvious to ignore; when they pulled his rap sheet and saw his 1971 rape and attempted rape charges, it was enough for a warrant.

And then another body turned up by the Knik River. Exotic dancer Paula Goulding, 30, had been missing since April: when she was found she too had been shot in the back with a .223 rifle and re-dressed after her death.

On 27 October 1983, Robert Hansen was arrested at his bakery, and detectives searched his home, his car and his plane. As well as finding a Ruger .223-calibre hunting rifle under his floorboards, a hidden compartment behind wood panelling revealed a cache of cheap jewellery – trophies from each of the women he had murdered. Most damning was an aviation map of the region around Anchorage, carefully marked with 24 hand-drawn asterisks. Four of them corresponded exactly to the spots where Joanne Messina, Ekluta Annie, Sherry Morrow and Paula Goulding had been found.

If the presence of so many asterisks was a sickening indication to investigators that their suspect might have been responsible for more murders than they had dared imagine, once Hansen explained how he would trick and then abduct his victims before setting them loose in the wilderness and hunting them down like animals, they could scarcely comprehend the scale of his depravities.

Robert Hansen eventually admitted to the murders of 17

women and of raping another 30 between 1971 and 1983 – though he insisted he had not killed Celia van Zanten, despite an 'x' on his map matching the location of her corpse. In 1984 he was sentenced to 461 years in prison without the possibility of parole.

As part of a plea bargain to serve his sentence in a federal prison, he showed investigators the precise locations of 17 grave sites – but refused to say anything more about the remaining seven asterisks on his map. He died behind bars in August 2014 without ever revealing what horrors might be found there.

PART THREE

KILLING
FOR KICKS

15

RETA MAYS

(USA, 2017–18, 7–20 VICTIMS)

It took two years for the FBI to prove that Reta Mays was a killer.

In July of 2018 the agency launched an official investigation after military veterans at the Louis A. Johnson Veterans Medical Center in Clarksburg, West Virginia, mysteriously started dying after suffering sudden and acute drops in their blood sugar levels. Seven had passed away within a year of each other; four of them died in a little over two weeks in March and April 2018.

Mays, a 43-year-old nursing assistant at the hospital who had previously worked as a prison officer and served with the National Guard in Iraq and Kuwait, was a person of interest from the start. But it would take a 24-month investigation that encompassed more than 300 interviews – including several with Mays herself – as well as an exhaustive review of phone, internet and social media history, the examination of thousands of pages of medical records and even the exhumation of some of the victims' bodies, before she was arrested.

When she finally admitted murdering seven of the veterans, including men who had served in Vietnam, the Korean War and the Second World War, she insisted that she had done so in order to help them pass away peacefully. The judge disagreed, describing her as a 'monster'.

A monster she may have been, but she is also almost unique among those who become forever defined by their murders.

Most serial killers are men. Whether this is for physiological or psychological reasons remains a point of debate, but broadly speaking, when women murder and murder and murder again, it is usually in connection with, or under the coercion of, a man. Where there are recognized female serial killers, such as Aileen Wuornos, their motives tend to be rage, or revenge. The methodical, cold-hearted, premeditated and ruthless killing of multiple victims remains something, by and large, that only men do.

Reta Mays is an exception that proves the rule.

*

Born in 1975 in the tiny rural community of Reynoldsville, near the town of Clarksburg, West Virginia, she joined the West

Virginia National Guard aged 25 and served for four years in the 1092nd Engineer Battalion, including tours in the Gulf in the aftermath of the Iraq War.

Nothing about her time in the National Guard gave any indication of the killer she would become, though Iraq in 2003 and 2004 was still highly volatile and life for the US forces stationed there extremely dangerous. During her time in the country, Mays would have learned how cheaply life can be valued – and how horrific death can be.

In 2005 she was discharged and returned to West Virginia, taking a position as a correctional officer at North Central Regional Jail, just a few miles from her birthplace, as well as becoming a regular at her local Methodist church.

She worked for seven years at the jail; a year after she left, an inmate filed a lawsuit against the institution, claiming he had suffered regular beatings and other abuse at the hands of several officers, including Mays. According to his statement, she had kicked him, 'bent over him, spit [sic] in his face, and said "How do you like that motherfucker? . . . You ain't that tough now are you?"'

The suit was nevertheless dismissed before it could come to trial, and after a stint working in a care home for adults with disabilities, in 2015 Mays took up a position as a nursing assistant at the Louis A. Johnson Veterans Medical Center, a hospital dedicated to helping former members of the armed forces, many of whom were elderly and needed round-the-clock supervision.

Her duties were basic – with no nursing qualifications

or licence to care for patients, her job was mostly one of observation, as well as measuring vital signs and testing blood glucose levels. In July 2017 she was assigned to work the night shift on Ward 3A of the hospital's medical surgical unit.

Meanwhile, her home life was unravelling. As well as the lingering North Central allegations, in 2012 her husband, Gordon Mays, had been jailed on child pornography charges, after pleading guilty to accessing dozens of images and videos of child abuse. In the small, close-knit, religious community of rural West Virginia, his jailing was big news; Reta stood by him, but in doing so found herself the subject of whispers, rumours, and the disapproval of many members of her Methodist church.

Within weeks of her starting on the night shift, Robert Edge Sr, an 82-year-old US Navy veteran of the Korean War, was rushed to the emergency room after a sudden and acute drop in his blood sugar level, bringing on a medical condition known as hypoglycaemia. He did not recover, and died on 20 July.

*

Robert Edge's rapid hypoglycaemic episode did not happen naturally. As he slept in the ward the previous night, Reta Mays had injected him with a fatally high dose of insulin stolen from the hospital's medications room. He likely died in agony.

Six months later she repeated the trick; in January 2018 Korean War veteran Robert Kozul, 89, also experienced an unexpected and catastrophic hypoglycaemic episode – once again, doctors were mystified as to how it could have happened.

Mays only waited two months before selecting her next victim – and then embarked upon a 16-day rush of killing in which four more veterans would fall prey to her night-time administrations.

On 23 March, Archie Edgell, an 84-year-old who had also served in Korea, suffered a dramatic crash in his blood sugar level. Doctors managed to stabilize him, before his levels plummeted again the following day. He never recovered, and his autopsy later found that he had been injected four times before dying: after failing to kill him with her first attempt, Mays had returned to see the job done properly.

Two days later George Shaw Sr, 81, also died unexpectedly of hypoglycaemia, and on 4 April his death was followed by that of William Holloway, 96, who had seen active service in the Second World War. The following week 82-year-old Vietnam War veteran Felix McDermott also passed away after an acute hypoglycaemic attack.

On 4 June, Raymond Golden, 88, who had served in the Army and Air Force in Korea and Vietnam, became the seventh patient at the hospital to experience a fatal blood sugar crash in just 11 months.

Although all the men who had died were elderly, none were undergoing end-of-life care, and all were expected to recover from the conditions that had seen them admitted to hospital in the first place.

Two weeks later an eighth man also fell ill with sudden hypoglycaemia: doctors managed to save 92-year-old Russell R. Posey Sr, who had fought in the US Navy in the Second

World War . . . but only for a short while. He later died at a nursing home on 3 July.

If staff and management at the medical centre were initially bewildered by the unexpected deaths of some of their most elderly patients, by the time of Russell Posey Sr's crash, there was a growing dread that all eight men had been the victims of a murderer, and that the killer was to be found within the hospital itself.

An internal investigation had already begun; in July 2018 it was turned over to the FBI, working alongside the United States Department for Veterans Affairs.

'We were informed in late June 2018 of possible suspicious deaths at the medical centre,' Michael Missal, Veterans Affairs Inspector General, revealed later. 'Within 24 hours we had a team on the ground and within days we identified Reta Mays as a person of interest.'

Mays was fired from her position at the hospital, but, for the time being at least, remained a free woman. She may have been the investigators' prime suspect, but they wanted the case against her to be watertight before making their move.

From the day she left the hospital, there were no further blood sugar crashes.

*

For months the investigating team dug deep into the medical history of each of the eight victims, looking for any clue or reason other than foul play for their deaths, conducting hundreds of interviews, reviewing thousands of pages of medical notes, and even exhuming some of the bodies for further examination.

They found nothing natural about the way they died. All of the veterans had perished after being injected with lethal doses of insulin, a medication used to regulate blood sugar levels in diabetics. Most of them had not even been prescribed insulin in the first place.

What's more, all had experienced their blood sugar crashes during nights when Reta Mays had been working – and in many cases, she had remained present as doctors struggled to save them, sometimes even lingering in the room as the news of their deaths was broken to their families.

As a night-shift nursing assistant Mays was not authorized to dispense medications, but the investigators quickly discovered that security at the medical centre was shockingly lax – and the medication room in which insulin was kept was often left unlocked. From Ward 3A Mays could effectively wander in and out of the room at will, and in the small hours of the night, unnoticed.

Mays was looking increasingly guilty of the murders, but with no fingerprints, eyewitnesses, discarded syringes or other forensic giveaways, the evidence against her remained purely circumstantial. The investigators kept digging.

FBI agents had interviewed Mays along with all the other hospital staff within days of opening the investigation. Now, armed with their circumstantial evidence, they tried again; she denied everything and revealed nothing.

In the meantime, agents delved deeper into her phone and

internet search records – and the results were chilling. Over the same months that patients had been suddenly dying on her watch, she had run Google searches for information on other female serial killers, and binge-watched the Netflix series *Nurses Who Kill* – one episode of which was devoted to insulin killings.

When investigators learned that Reta's husband was in prison, they also pulled the recorded phone conversations she had with him throughout 2017 and 2018, in which she frequently moaned about the patients she looked after.

In one call, made the morning after one of the blood sugar crashes, she told him: 'At four o'clock in the morning I had to take over sitting in one of the one-on-ones . . . and the one I was sitting with I wanted to freaking strangle.'

In another she complained of having to help resuscitate a patient.

'He couldn't do anything for himself,' she said, 'He had to be fed, everything. He had no quality of life and last week if they would have just said DNR [Do Not Resuscitate] he would have went to sleep when his blood sugar dropped down to 30. He would have just went to sleep and not woke up.'

A blood sugar reading of less than 70 is considered harmful; anything below 55 is seriously dangerous.

'We checked his blood sugar . . . and he was 258 – so it wasn't his blood sugar this time,' she continued, before laughing.

If the agents were intrigued by an untrained nursing assistant's apparently detailed knowledge of blood sugar levels, it was the words 'this time' and the laugh that sent shivers down their spines.

A year after her second interview Mays was asked to come in again. This time another agent, who had a similar military background to Mays', talked to her for more than six hours in an effort to get her to confess. She remained tight-lipped, but immediately after the grilling requested an attorney – and investigators finally had their way in.

*

Reta Mays may have been prepared to deny and deny again, but once her lawyers were presented with the mountain of evidence accumulated by the investigating team, they convinced her that she would almost certainly lose if it came to a jury trial. In July 2020 she entered a plea of guilty to the murders of Archie Edgell, Robert Edge, Robert Kozul, George Shaw, William Holloway, Felix McDermott and Raymond Golden. As part of a plea deal, she was only charged with the attempted murder of Russell Posey.

The court also heard something like a justification, or at least explanation, for her actions. She wanted to help the elderly veterans that she felt were suffering, she said. She gave them lethal insulin injections so they could pass away 'peacefully'.

They did not die peacefully, or even quickly. As their blood sugar levels plummeted, their organs gradually shut down, resulting in long, slow, agonizing deaths.

Assistant US Attorney Jarod Douglas was not buying her justification. 'Apparently the defendant found some excitement or self-worth in causing these emergencies,' he told the judge.

'These actions gave the defendant a sense of control.'

With her husband in prison on child pornography charges and in the face of the stigma she received in her small community as the wife of a convicted paedophile, it may have been that Reta Mays had sought to manufacture some kind of self-worth by being present at the death of others and helping to console their families – even to the point of causing those deaths.

Or it may be that the same scorn with which she allegedly viewed the inmates at North Central Regional Jail extended to the frail old men who she was charged to look after, even when she wanted to 'freaking strangle' them.

Or it may be that she simply enjoyed killing. Although investigators and FBI agents formally linked her to the eight deaths between July 2017 and June 2018, they have stated that they believe there may have been as many as 20 victims of the woman the press would dub 'the Angel of Death'.

None of the murders were committed in a fit of rage, or out of a lust for revenge; all were calculated, careful, deliberate and premeditated. As the judge sentenced Reta Mays to seven consecutive life sentences plus 20 years in prison, he addressed her directly.

'Several times your counsels made the point that you shouldn't be considered a monster,' he said. 'Respectfully, I disagree with that. You are the worst kind. You're the monster that no one sees coming.'

16

PAUL JOHN KNOWLES

(USA, 1974, 18–35 VICTIMS)

When Dawn Wine, a pretty and popular 16-year-old from Marlborough, Connecticut, heard the knock on her door, she had no reason to be alarmed. Although the October nights were drawing in, it was still only 5pm, and the area in which she lived – all leafy streets and large, detached houses – was almost totally crime-free.

She remained unconcerned after she opened the door. Standing in her driveway was a tall, slim, ruggedly handsome man with collar-length red hair; he smiled and asked if her mother was home. Not until six when she clocks off from work, she replied. Perhaps your father, then? Dawn explained that he no longer lived with them and could she help?

He smiled again – and then shoved her hard backwards into the house, stepped smartly inside, shut the door behind him and pulled a sawed-off shotgun from his trousers. He was on top of Dawn before she could regain her feet, forcing a gag into her mouth and pushing her upstairs into her bedroom.

Still pointing the shotgun at the terrified teenager, he told her to strip naked, before binding her wrists and ankles and sexually assaulting her on her own bed. As he raped her he spoke to her softly, gently, reassuring her that he was not there to hurt her.

An hour later Dawn's mother Karen arrived home from her job at the local hospital. The man was waiting for her, shotgun in hand, with Dawn, now dressed again, beside him. Once again, speaking in a soft southern drawl, he explained that he was not there to harm anyone, but sure would appreciate some dinner before going on his way.

Despite the friendly tone, it was not a request so much as an order; and for the next surreal few hours, the three played out a perverse form of happy families, mother and daughter cooking before the three ate together at the dining table, shotgun at his feet.

After thanking them for the delicious meal, he told them there was just one more thing he wanted to do before leaving: he appreciated it was frightening, but he had to insist on tying them up, just so they could not raise the alarm too soon after his departure. He would bind each of them in their bedrooms, if they didn't mind? Oh, and they would have to strip first.

When their bodies were found days later, Karen and Dawn

were lying face down on their beds with their hands tied behind their backs. Both had been raped, and both had been strangled with knotted nylon stockings. The only thing missing from their house was a portable tape recorder.

*

It was never conclusively proved that Paul John Knowles was responsible for the murders of Karen and Dawn Wine, but in a series of eloquent, detailed, if boastful, taped confessions he gave to his lawyer – and which were most likely recorded on the very same machine he took from their house – he claimed that the mother and daughter were his twelfth and thirteenth victims in a haphazard and apparently motiveless rampage that spanned at least seven states in the space of just four months in late 1974.

He was eventually tied to the murders of 18 men, women and children; he claimed the true number to be anything up to 35.

His frantic four-month killing spree was not an organized or methodical process – it was a messy, amoral, senseless riot of violence. There was no plan behind the slayings, no fixation on a particular type of target or reason for targeting them.

His victims had little in common, they spanned ages from seven to 65 years old, and they were a mix of male and female. Some were the subject of home invasions, others were met and spontaneously killed on the road. Some were strangled, some stabbed, some shot; some he sexually abused, some he did not; some he stole from, others were murdered for no apparent reason.

Knowles was a serial killer with no pattern to his killings – and because of the erratic nature of his methods and the differences in his targets, it was not until police heard his own taped confessions that they were even aware his victims had all been killed by the same man.

When his identity was finally known, the press dubbed him the 'Casanova Killer' – due in part to his smouldering good looks, but also because his rampage began after he charmed, and was then rejected by, a woman who promised to marry him before they had even met.

*

Paul John Knowles's wild four months of violence and murder began and ended with attempted escapes from police custody. The first was successful; the second ended in his own death.

Born in Florida in April 1946, Knowles had a fractured childhood, and was raised in a series of foster homes. Although highly intelligent – his IQ was recorded as 129, which is bordering on 'gifted' – he was a disruptive influence from the start, regularly running into trouble with the law throughout his teens.

His first incarceration came when he was 19, when he was jailed for kidnapping a police officer. For the following eight years he would spend roughly six months of each year behind bars as he drifted around Florida and Georgia, stealing cars and committing burglary.

It was while serving one of his sentences at Raiford prison in

Florida that he began a bizarre relationship with Angela Covic, a divorced cocktail waitress from San Francisco who had written to him through a pen-pal scheme. She was initially drawn in by the eloquence and intelligence of his letters – but after he sent her a photograph she was fully smitten. His rugged, angular face and long, tousled hair had the look of movie stars like Robert Redford and Ryan O'Neal; within months she accepted his proposal of marriage and paid for a lawyer to win him a parole appeal, as well as an airline ticket to fly out to California.

In May 1974 she met him at the airport – and immediately called off the wedding. In person he was if anything even better looking than his photos, but the charming, sensitive, eloquent man whose letters she had obsessed over gave her a very different impression in the flesh: she later described him as having an 'aura of fear' that shocked and frightened her.

She fled, and a furious Knowles was suddenly denied the doting woman he thought was going to pay all his bills from then on. He later claimed to have murdered three random people on the streets of San Francisco that night in revenge.

After returning to Florida he managed just a few more months before once again running into trouble – an argument with a bartender in Jacksonville turned violent, and then near-deadly, as Knowles pulled a knife. The man was not seriously injured, but Knowles was arrested and held in a police cell.

This time he had had enough of being kept behind bars. As officers settled down for the night, he picked the lock of his cell, and on 26 July 1974, broke out. Within hours he started killing in earnest.

The first to die was 65-year-old Jacksonville resident Alice Curtis. Almost immediately after escaping from jail, Knowles broke into her house, tied her up and choked her to death, before ransacking the property for valuables and making off in her car.

Six days later, according to his taped confessions, he was trying to lie low – already wanted for his jailbreak, Jacksonville police had also connected him to the Curtis murder – when he ran into sisters Lillian Annette and Mylette Josephine Anderson, aged 11 and 7 respectively, who recognized him from his picture on the local news reports. Worried they might go to the police, he snatched them off the street, strangled them in the back of his stolen car and dumped their bodies in a swamp outside town for the alligators to dispose of. Their remains have never been recovered.

The following day Knowles broke into the home of 49-year-old Marjorie Howie in nearby Atlantic Beach, strangling her with a knotted nylon stocking and stealing her television set.

After just one week on the run, Knowles had killed four times – but if the murders were shocking, they could at least be viewed through the lens of motive. Marjorie Howie and Alice Curtis were killed because he needed money; the Anderson girls were the tragic casualties of a desperate man on the run.

After 2 August, however, Knowles's victims were no longer murdered out of any sense of necessity, no matter how twisted. For the next three and a half months, killing became something he did for its own sake.

As he fled Florida and drifted north and west across the

country, he left a trail of devastation in his wake. Thirteen-year-old Ima Sanders was picked up hitchhiking in Georgia, strangled, raped and dumped in the woods; and on 23 August, Knowles forced his way into the Georgia home of Kathie Pearce, 24, where he strangled her with a telephone cord while her three-year-old son watched. He left the child unharmed.

On 3 September he met businessman William Bates, 32, in a bar near Lima, Ohio. After striking up a conversation the pair left together; a month later Bates's naked body would be found in nearby woods. Knowles had strangled him and stolen his car.

Two weeks afterwards, in Nevada, some 2,400 miles from Jacksonville, he murdered elderly campers Emmett and Lois Johnson by a rest stop near the town of Ely; three days later, now in Texas, he stopped to 'help' 42-year-old Ebon Hicks, whose car had broken down. She was raped, strangled, and her body left by the side of the road like trash.

In Alabama he met 49-year-old beautician Ann Jean Dawson, whom he charmed into accompanying him on his feverish road trip across the southern states. For a week they travelled together, with Dawson paying the bills, before he grew tired of her. On 29 September he strangled her and threw her body into the Mississippi River. Her remains would not be found for another three years.

By mid-October he had arrived in Virginia, where he broke into the home of 53-year-old Doris Hovey. She was shot with her husband's rifle, and the weapon placed beside her as a staged suicide. There was no evidence of sexual assault and nothing had been taken from the house.

Doris Hovey's murder came two days after the rape and murder of Karen and Dawn Wine in Connecticut, 400 miles to the north. Although both were apparently motiveless, senselessly cruel killings in which nothing of value had been taken, there was no reason for investigators in the separate states to connect the killings to each other, or to any of the other random homicides that had happened across the country in the preceding weeks.

But it would be the one item that Knowles had taken from those two most recent crime scenes that would eventually bring to light the true scale of his murder spree. Once again in Florida, he had picked up two hitchhikers with the intention of murdering them, but he was almost immediately pulled over for a traffic violation. Although the policeman let him off with a warning, he was shaken – and called his lawyer for advice.

The lawyer told him to turn himself in. Knowles didn't like the sound of that, but did the next best thing, and – most probably using the tape machine he had stolen from the Wines' house – made a series of audio recordings in which he described all of his murders.

He mailed the tapes to his lawyer, and days later killed again.

On 6 November, Carswell Carr, 45, met Knowles in a bar in Milledgeville, Georgia; after the younger man admitted that he was drifting from motel to motel, Carr took pity on him and invited him back to his home, where he could get a proper meal and a good night's sleep.

The following day, when Carr's wife Ellen returned from her night shift at the hospital, she found a scene of almost unimaginable horror. The mutilated corpse of her husband was sprawled across their bedroom floor: he had been stabbed 27 times with a pair of scissors and what was left of him trussed with a curtain cord. In the next room was the body of their 15-year-old daughter Mandy, face down on her bed, strangled to death with a nylon stocking still tied around her neck and with another stuffed down her throat. There was also evidence that she had been sexually violated after her death.

The local paper described the killings as 'one of the most brutal murders in recent middle Georgia history', and the police chief told reporters that it was probably the work of more than one killer, and that they were 'maniacs'.

Two days later, Knowles met British journalist Sandy Fawkes in Atlanta, Georgia, and the pair enjoyed a two-day romance together, which she would document in her book *Killing Time*, subsequently retitled *Natural Born Killer*. Intriguingly, as well as describing his movie star looks, Fawkes claimed that Knowles was impotent, and unable to have sex with her.

Their fling ended on 10 November, and four days later Knowles broke into the West Palm Beach home of sisters Beverley and Barbara Mabee and abducted Barbara, making off in her car. Barbara was later released alive, but the following morning Florida Highway Patrol trooper Charles Campbell recognized the stolen car near the town of Perry, 350 miles to the north.

As the trooper pulled the car over, Knowles acted fast, drawing his shotgun and knocking Campbell's weapon away before he could react. Campbell was cuffed, and the pair made off in the patrol car, using the siren to flag down another vehicle, into which Knowles bundled the policeman, before speeding off again.

After crossing into Georgia, Knowles took both his hostages into the woods, bound them together around a tree and calmly shot each of them in the head.

*

For four months Paul John Knowles had run riot across America, raping, assaulting and killing at will in a manic and seemingly motiveless orgy of violence. But if detectives across the seven separate states in which he had murdered had still not joined the dots, he was now wanted for the abduction and murder of a police officer.

Patrols and roadblocks were set up across Georgia and before long his car was spotted in Henry County, just south of Atlanta. A frantic chase began, and as Knowles tried to crash through a roadblock, he span out of control, smashing into a tree.

Somehow he got out alive and set off on foot into the woods, pursued by more than 200 police officers with dogs, as well as air support from helicopters. He was finally cornered and, on 17 November, once again put behind bars.

Once in custody, Knowles not only came clean, he did so with swagger, claiming that as well as the 18 murders that could be verified as his doing, he was responsible for the same number again that the authorities did not know about. There was no remorse, no regret; his calm self-assurance was unnerving, almost as if he didn't feel the game was ended just yet.

On 18 December 1974, the Casanova Killer played his final hand.

After telling detectives that he would lead them to a spot in the Georgia woods where he had hidden one of his murder weapons, he once again attempted a dramatic escape. As they drove along the freeway he picked the lock of his handcuffs with a stolen paperclip, and made a grab for one of the officers' guns.

This time he was not quick enough. As Knowles lunged for the weapon, Agent Ronnie Angel from the Georgia Bureau of Investigation reacted first, slamming three shots from his own gun into Knowles's chest at point-blank range. He died instantly.

Paul John Knowles was just 28 when he died, and for the final four months of his life had dramatically reinvented himself from drifting low-level burglar to one of America's most vicious and senseless serial killers.

His early death means we shall never know just what it was that made the handsome, intelligent man with an IQ of 129 go so devastatingly off the rails, but in Sandy Fawkes's book about her brief fling with the killer, he gives her an eerily prophetic clue.

'I haven't got long to live,' he told her. 'I am going to be killed. Soon. It might be in two days or in two months. I don't know when, but within a year I shall be dead. I am going to be killed by someone.'

17

JOANNA CHRISTINE DENNEHY

(UK, 2013, 3 VICTIMS)

In February 2014, Joanna Dennehy became only the third woman in the UK to be given a whole-life-tariff prison sentence, following in the bloody footsteps of Myra Hindley in 1966 and Rosemary West in 1995. But where Hindley and West murdered under the supervision, control or coercion of a dominant male partner, Dennehy's murders were entirely her own. She had male accomplices, but there is no question about who was in charge: after killing for a third time, she instructed friend Gary Stretch to help her find more victims, telling him: 'I want my fun. I need you to get my fun.'

She remained defiantly unapologetic after her arrest and during her trial shocked her own legal team by entering a surprise guilty plea. As her lawyers asked the judge for a delay in proceedings to check that she really wanted to admit to the murders, she interrupted: 'I've pleaded guilty and that's that. I'm not coming back down here again just to say the same stuff. It's a long way to come to say the same thing I have just said.'

Before leaving the court room she was seen laughing.

If 'monster' is an overused and sometimes reductively simple word used to describe serial killers, it is not so in Joanna Dennehy's case. Her crimes are inexplicable, her reasons for killing essentially meaningless.

In March 2013 she stabbed to death three men in ten days, two of them within hours of each other. Their bodies were dumped in ditches, one of them dressed in a black sequinned dress and his corpse arranged so his buttocks were exposed. Three days later she attempted to kill another two men as they walked their dogs. She later described the act of murder as 'moreish', adding that after her first killing she 'got a taste for it'.

She might be called a nihilist, or a narcissist, or a hedonist, addicted to the thrill of taking a life just for the sake of it – but ultimately, her sad, sordid story really is simply the tale of a monster.

When psychiatrists asked her why she killed her three victims, her answer was frighteningly dismissive. 'They shouldn't have pissed me off,' she said.

*

When Kevin Lee first met the woman who would later murder him, he was both a little intimidated and a little excited by her. The 48-year-old ran a business letting out rooms to homeless and vulnerable people in Peterborough, eastern England – a devoted husband and father of two, he was known as a kind man, always looking to see the best in people, no matter their backgrounds or circumstances.

In early 2013 Joanna Dennehy had been referred to him by the council as someone looking for a place to stay. When she admitted that she had only recently been released from prison, he was unconcerned – so had many of his other tenants. What was important in his eyes was giving them a chance to get back on their feet and start afresh. When she told him that her sentence had been eight years for killing her father after he raped her, and that she had killed another two people in a house fire and a further two by running them over in her car, he was a little more wary, but stuck to his principles. She deserved another chance, he resolved, and he gave her a room in one of his properties.

Over the following weeks his kindness towards her grew into something more like fascination. Dennehy had a vibrancy, an energy about her; she did things on her own uncompromising terms and refused to be daunted by anyone, man or woman. Although she was only five foot five, the 31-year-old carried herself with a poise and swagger; he soon gave her work helping carry out repairs on his bedsits, later using her as a rent collector. Accompanied by her friends Gary Stretch, a seven-foot giant of a man, and Leslie Layton, both petty burglars who also had rooms in Lee's properties, Dennehy's methods were basic, but effective. Late payers were threatened with violence; persistent late payers were told she would 'fucking kill them'. They believed her too.

She was also uncompromisingly open about her sexuality, telling Lee how she enjoyed casual relations with both men and women, often involving sadomasochistic role play, and showing him scars on her arms where she had cut herself during sex to heighten the experience. Even the star tattoo she had under her right eye held a dangerously erotic quality – she had inked it herself, she told him, cutting the design into her face with a knife.

By the spring of 2013 Lee was near-infatuated, telling friends Dennehy reminded him of Uma Thurman in the movie *Kill Bill*, and when she invited him to her bedsit on the night of 29 March, he did not hesitate before accepting.

Once inside she poured the drinks, and as the pair grew more intimate, she produced a sequinned dress, and a knife. 'Put it on,' she told him, 'I want to dress you up and rape you'.

As he changed, she attacked.

Before he knew what was happening, Dennehy was all over him. With a strength that belied her slim frame she slammed the blade again and again into his chest, tearing through flesh, shearing through bone, slicing through his lungs and, eventually, fatally puncturing his heart. As he bled to death, she laughed at the ridiculous sight of his lifeless body in the sequinned dress, before calling her friends Stretch and Layton to help her clear up.

When they arrived they found not only Lee's body, but also that of John Chapman, a 56-year-old Falklands veteran who had fallen on hard times and turned to alcohol. He was a fellow resident in the same building that contained Dennehy's bedsit, and was a persistent late payer – she had previously told him that she would get him out of the house 'by any means'.

Just hours before she had seduced and then slaughtered Lee, Chapman had also been invited for a drink – though she didn't waste any time pretending she wanted to have sex with him. Despite Chapman's background serving in the Navy, years of alcohol abuse had ravaged his body, and she quickly overpowered him, killing him with six deep stabs in the chest.

It's doubtful that Stretch and Layton were even surprised by the dead bodies. Ten days earlier they had been called to do a similar disposal and clean-up job at the flat.

Dennehy had met 31-year-old Polish immigrant Lukasz Slaboszewski among the drug users and homeless of Peterborough; although he had found work in a local warehouse, he was still sleeping rough or in shelters, and had become entranced by the magnetic woman with the star tattoo. On 19 March she sent him a series of flirtatious text messages inviting him over; he told friends that he was going to meet his new girlfriend.

Once Slaboszewski was inside her flat she took him into the kitchen, and as he poured the drinks, she told him she wanted him to wear a blindfold when they had sex.

The moment his eyes were covered she attacked him with her knife, stabbing him first in the kitchen before dragging him through to the living room where she continued slashing and tearing at him with the blade until he was dead.

Stretch was then summoned, and the pair dumped the body in a wheelie bin outside the house. Two days later, using money borrowed from Kevin Lee, Dennehy, Stretch and Layton bought a second-hand car, took the body out to a spot in the countryside 10 miles to the east of the city, and left it in a ditch.

John Chapman's corpse would join it a little over a week later; Kevin Lee's remains were left a short distance away near the village of Newborough. And after telling Stretch, 'I want my fun,' Dennehy went in search of more victims.

*

There was nothing in Joanna Dennehy's early upbringing to suggest the horrors that would later unfold, or the deeply disturbing psychological issues that would eventually propel her to seek pleasure in harming herself and others.

Far from the tale she told Kevin Lee, her father did not rape her, and she did not murder him, but was instead raised in a comfortable middle-class suburb near the affluent town of St Albans with her parents and younger sister Maria. She played for the school hockey and netball teams, did well in her exams and harboured ambitions of going to university to study law.

Aged 15, however, something changed. She met and fell in

love with John Treanor, a man five years her senior, and began drinking and taking drugs. The following year she quit school and ran away with him. Before she was 20 she was a mother twice over, and had become permanently estranged from her own parents after telling them they would have to pay if they wanted to see their grandchildren.

As she and Treanor moved from Luton to Milton Keynes and finally East Anglia, supporting themselves with whatever manual jobs they could get, her drinking and drug abuse worsened. With it came violence – most often directed at the man she now blamed for ruining her life. She also started carrying a knife, hiding it in her boots.

In 2009, fearful of her increasingly bad temper, Treanor took the children and fled to Manchester. He later told reporters: 'I really believe Jo is evil, pure and simple; that is why I took the girls as far away from her as possible.'

Now free of responsibilities, but also of any semblance of stability, Dennehy drifted around eastern England, working as a farm labourer, as well as stealing and turning to prostitution to fund her drink and drugs habits. She began self-harming, cutting her arms, stomach and neck and etching the star tattoo on her right cheek. She carried the obsession with pain into her increasingly promiscuous sex life; partners would be humiliated and hurt as part of the sexual act, and when she used her dagger to inflict cuts on herself during intercourse, she enjoyed the look of shock on their faces.

In 2012 she was arrested for assault and owning a dangerous dog, and shortly afterwards was given a 14-week prison sentence for theft. Immediately after her release she was admitted to hospital for psychiatric treatment, where she was diagnosed with an antisocial personality disorder and an obsessive compulsive disorder. She did not receive any counselling or treatment for either condition.

It was following her discharge from hospital that she turned up at Kevin Lee's door, looking for a place to stay. Her boasts of spending eight years in prison for the murder of her father and of killing four other men were fantasies . . . but it seems she was determined to make them a reality.

*

On 30 March 2013, Lee's body was found by a dog walker lying in a ditch near the motorway at Newborough. He had been deliberately arranged face down and with his buttocks exposed, still wearing the sequinned dress, as if to prolong his humiliation, even in death.

When police interviewed his distraught wife, she pointed the finger at the wayward, often frightening woman she suspected her husband of having an affair with, repeating the tale Lee had told her of Dennehy having killed five times before.

Police immediately headed towards the property that Dennehy shared with John Chapman and Leslie Layton. Neither Dennehy nor Chapman were anywhere to be found, though the flat stank of bleach, and a blood-stained mattress had been left outside the back door.

They did find Layton, however, and after examining his phone and finding a photo of a dead Chapman covered in blood, took him in for questioning.

Like Gary Stretch, Kevin Lee and Lukasz Slaboszewski, Layton may have fallen under Dennehy's spell, but he was not about to take a murder rap for her. Once in custody he explained how Dennehy had stabbed Lee to death – and how, after that, on seeing a report of his murder on the news, she had 'jumped around' delightedly, and sung the Britney Spears song, 'Oops! I did it again'.

When asked where Dennehy was now, he told police that she and Stretch had taken off in their car. He didn't know where.

On 2 April, they turned up in Hereford, 140 miles to the west.

Shortly after 3.30pm, retired firefighter Robin Bereza, 63, was walking home along Westfaling Street in the city, when he felt a sudden sharp pain in his back. He turned to see Dennehy, her knife already coated in his blood. As he staggered and fell, she stabbed him a second time, before leaving him for dead on the pavement, casually sauntering back to the car where Stretch, and another man whom they had forced to accompany them, were waiting.

Ten minutes later she struck again, approaching 56-year-old John Rogers, who was walking his dog in the nearby Belmont Estate. 'My boyfriend told me to do this,' she hissed, and launched a volley of strikes, stabbing and slicing at his back and chest more than 30 times, before jumping back into the car and speeding off again.

Miraculously, neither man was fatally injured, and after Rogers was spotted and emergency services called, Hereford police raced to find his assailant before she could attack anyone else.

It took just 19 minutes to track down Joanna Dennehy. When she was arrested she was sitting calmly outside a shop just a few minutes from the sites of her two attempted murders. She handed over her knife without a struggle, and as she was booked into the station laughed and flirted with the arresting officers.

*

The next day the bodies of Chapman and Slaboszewski were found, and in November Dennehy pleaded guilty to all three murders. Stretch received a life sentence for his part in assisting her, and Layton was sentenced to 14 years' imprisonment.

Dennehy never expressed any remorse for her crimes, or even real interest in the men she had killed and injured. At her trial it was revealed that she had told her accomplices that she wanted to kill nine men in total, because that was how many American gangsters Bonnie and Clyde had murdered.

'This case is unique and unprecedented,' David Wilson, professor of criminology at Birmingham University, told the *Guardian* newspaper after her sentencing. 'There was never any sense of her disengaging. She seems to have constantly been in the moment of killing . . . So often it is the woman who follows the world view of the more dominant male partner. In this case Dennehy was the dominant partner.'

Her sister Maria put it more bluntly: 'She likes people to know she's the boss.'

18

IVAN MILAT

(AUSTRALIA, 1989–93, 7+ VICTIMS)

For Joanne Walters and Caroline Clarke it was supposed to be the experience of a lifetime. Joanne, from Wales, was 22 and had taken time out from her job as a nanny to travel round Australia. Almost immediately after arriving in the country, she had met 21-year-old Caroline, from Northumberland, and the pair hit it off immediately.

For weeks in the long hot Australian summer of 1992 they had followed the trail of thousands of other young people who flocked to that country each year, travelling on work visas, thumbing lifts between cities, enjoying the sunshine, hospitality and easy-going, friendly vibe that made Australia the hottest destination for so many British backpackers and gap-year students.

By the autumn they had made it to Sydney, and shared a cheap flat together in the city's vibrant Kings Cross district; and on Easter Saturday, 18 April, they set off again, hitching south and west to pick fruit in Victoria. Their last confirmed sighting was at Kings Cross station, both loaded with rucksacks and sleeping bags. Another witness later claimed to have seen two young women matching their description 50 miles south, near the town of Wollongong, heading for the interstate highway.

Joanne Walters and Caroline Clarke would not be seen alive again.

Five months later, on 19 September, two men orienteering in the Belanglo State Forest, a wild, unspoilt area of bushland just off the interstate to the south-east of Wollongong, stumbled upon what they thought was the corpse of a kangaroo. As they drew closer, they realized it was something far worse – the decomposing remains of a human body. The next morning, police uncovered a second cadaver just 100 feet away.

Despite the decomposition, forensic examiners were able to identify the bodies as those of Walters and Clarke. Both had been bound, sexually abused and stabbed. Walters had suffered four stab wounds to the chest, one to the neck, and nine in the back, including one wound to her upper spine that would have paralysed her. In addition to her other injuries, Clarke had been shot 10 times in the head; police surmised that she had been used as target practice.

The site was also littered with discarded cigarette butts and shell cartridges from a Ruger 10/22 rifle – by their number, investigators concluded that the women's killer had taken his time with his victims. This was no frenzied attack, but rather a prolonged, agonizing torture.

A year later more corpses were found.

On 5 October 1993, a man camping in the Belanglo Forest unearthed what looked like human bones while gathering firewood. When police arrived they found another two bodies, a male and a female. They were identified as Deborah Everist and her boyfriend James Gibson, two 19-year-olds from Victoria who had last been seen on 30 December 1989, leaving Sydney to hitch along the interstate to a festival.

Like Walters and Clarke, they too had suffered horrific agonies before they died. Gibson was lying in a foetal position; he had been stabbed eight times in the lungs, heart and liver, as well as enduring another forceful slash across his back, severing his spine.

Everist, lying nearby, had her bra and pants removed and had been gagged and bound with her own tights. She had been stabbed once in the back and so savagely beaten that her jaw was smashed and her skull fractured in two places. There were also knife marks on her head.

Another missing backpacker, 21-year-old German Simone Schmidl, was discovered in Belanglo on 1 November. She had been stabbed eight times: two of the blows had severed her spine, the others had punctured her heart and lungs. She had last been seen on 20 January 1991, after telling friends she planned to hitchhike from Sydney to Melbourne.

Three days later, the bodies of two more missing German tourists were found. Twenty-one-year-old Gabor Neugebauer and his girlfriend Anja Habschied, 20, had disappeared after leaving Kings Cross on 26 December 1991, heading for Victoria.

They were lying just half a mile from Schmidl's remains. Gabor was fully clothed and had been tied, gagged and strangled before being shot six times in the head. Only Anja's torso was found; pathologists determined that she had been forced to kneel with her head bowed before being decapitated while still alive. Her skull has never been recovered.

In all cases, forensic examination showed that few of the victims died quickly. All seven had been tortured, perhaps for hours, and probably died slowly from their injuries, bleeding out into the forest floor while their tormentor smoked cigarettes and listened to their feeble pleas for mercy.

*

Seven young men and women had been found dead in the Belanglo Forest in a little over a year. The similarities between the killings were obvious – apart from the fact that all had last been reported hitching lifts along the interstate between Sydney and Victoria, the leisurely nature of their murders, with their killer clearly enjoying stringing out their deaths for as long as possible, and details such as the severing of their spinal cords and the 'target practice' inflicted upon Caroline Clarke and Gabor Neugebauer, left police in no doubt that there was a serial killer on the loose in New South Wales.

Not only a serial killer, but a particularly brutal and sadistic serial killer, preying on the trusting nature of young backpackers, upon whom he would inflict near-unimaginable horrors. A huge operation was put into place, and investigators reviewed what they knew for sure.

Given the remote nature of the forest and surrounding area, the killer almost certainly drove a four-wheel-drive truck, and was familiar with the lesser-known bush tracks; he would also be physically strong enough to overwhelm and restrain pairs of victims at a time; and he owned several large knives or machetes, as well as a US-made Ruger 10/22 rifle – a gun that was relatively rare in Australia at the time.

As the travellers had all gone missing while hitching along the interstate from Sydney, detectives worked on the assumption that their killer either lived in Sydney itself or close to the highway south-west of the city.

Beyond that . . . nothing.

The day after Neugebauer and Habschied's bodies were found, a reward for half a million Australian dollars was posted for information leading to the killer's conviction – at the time the biggest sum offered in Australian history. Confidential tip lines were set up, and as the nation reeled from the barbarity of the killings, within 24 hours over 5,000 calls were logged. The final tally would exceed 1 million.

A week later, on 13 November, among the deluge of information came a call from the UK. Paul Onions, a 24-year-old engineer from Birmingham, had seen the reports of the murders in the British newspapers and had some information he thought might be helpful. He told police how in January 1990 he had been backpacking in New South Wales and while making his way west from Sydney, had thumbed a lift from a man in a four-wheel-drive called Bill.

As they neared the Belanglo Forest, Bill had suddenly pulled the car over and pulled out a revolver. It wasn't the gun that scared him, Onions remembered, so much as the rope he saw sticking out of the man's bag. Without hesitating, he opened the door, jumped out of the vehicle, and ran for his life – even as Bill fired shots after him.

Onions got lucky. Running straight into the road, he flagged down a van, jumped into the back and screamed at the driver to put her foot down. They stopped at the nearest police station and filed a report, but he heard nothing more and soon afterwards left Australia to return to England.

Onions gave a description of his assailant, and detectives dug into the archives to uncover his original statement.

What they found looked like a lead. Paul Onions' description matched another tip they had received from the wife of a worker at a Sydney building materials plant. She had suspicions about one of the men her husband knew there. A man by the name of Milat.

*

Ivan Milat – one of 16 children to his Croatian emigrant father and Australian mother – was born into a large and impoverished farming family in the rural scrubland west of Sydney in 1944. Life for the Milats was hard, and he and his nine brothers grew up semi-wild, known to police for shooting guns and throwing knives at targets set up in the woods near their house.

By his early teens, Ivan's unruly behaviour led to a stint at a residential school; and later criminal convictions for theft, breaking and entering, and driving a stolen car culminated in a three-year prison sentence in 1967, when he was 22 years old. Soon after his release, he committed his most serious crime to date.

On 9 April 1971 Milat picked up two 18-year-old hitchhikers near Liverpool train station in Sydney and after pulling off the highway onto a dirt road, produced a knife. As the terrified girls begged to be let go, he tied them up before raping one of them on the front seat of his car.

Bizarrely, after the attack he then pulled the car back on to the main road and calmly drove to a service station, where he told them he would buy them each a fizzy drink. As he was inside they grabbed their chance and, their hands and feet still bound, struggled back onto the road, where they managed to escape in another car.

Milat was quickly arrested and charged with rape and armed robbery, but in 1974 he walked free from court, after one of the women changed her story and a jury believed his assertion that they had consented to sex.

It was to be Milat's last court appearance for two decades. The following year he appeared to have settled down, taking a job as a driver with the New South Wales Roads & Traffic Authority, and in 1984, marrying Karen Duck, who at 17 was 23 years his junior.

The newly respectable façade was nothing more than an illusion. On Valentine's Day 1987, Karen fled the marriage with their daughter, accusing him of beating her and describing him as 'gun crazy'.

Two years later their divorce was finalized, and backpackers began to go missing along the road south-west of Sydney.

*

By early 1994, the investigations into Ivan Milat that had begun with Paul Onions' long-distance call and the tip-off from a wife of a worker at the Roads & Traffic Authority had escalated into a serious line of inquiry.

Meticulously cross-checking all historical reports of attacks on travellers between Sydney and Victoria, detectives had unearthed Milat's arrest and trial for the 1971 assault and rape of the two hitchhikers.

They also learned that he had been absent from work on the days each of the seven backpackers had disappeared, and that he had hurriedly sold his Nissan four-by-four in the days following the discovery of Joanne Walters and Caroline Clarke.

They were still lacking a credible witness, however. On 2 May, Paul Onions was flown to Australia and interviewed again. He confirmed that his attacker had driven a four-by-four vehicle, that he sported a bushy moustache similar to the Australian cricketer Merv Hughes, and that before he had pulled the gun he had mentioned he was of a Yugoslav background. After detectives showed him a series of photographs of different men matching that description, Onions didn't hesitate – and pointed straight at Ivan Milat.

At a little after 6.30am on 22 May, 50 heavily armed police surrounded Milat's home and he was ordered to come out with his hands above his head. As he was cuffed and taken away, charged for the moment only with the attack on Onions, police searched the house.

Hidden around the building – or in some cases left out in plain sight – were trophies and mementoes from several of the murders. Simone Schmidl's water bottle and Caroline Clarke's camera were found, as well as Simone's tent and sleeping bag, and another sleeping bag belonging to Deborah Everist. In the garage was a pillowcase containing blood-stained sash cords, in his bedroom a stash of .22 cartridges and electrical tape matching that used at the murder scenes, and in the spare room a large Bowie knife, as well as a manual for the same rare Ruger 10/22 rifle that had killed Clarke and Neugebauer. Detectives also uncovered parts of the Ruger gun itself, as well as a map of the Belanglo Forest.

On 31 May 1994, Milat was charged with all seven backpacker murders; and in March 1996, as the trial began, he entered a plea of not guilty.

Over the course of 18 weeks, the full horror of Ivan Milat's crimes was revealed, as the court was told in graphic detail how he would torment his victims for hours, tying and untying them, moving them around his makeshift campsites in the forest, dressing and undressing them, and making them watch as he fired hundreds of shells at beer bottle targets, before taking aim at them.

The initial stab wounds would be directed at severing their spinal cords, leaving them alive and in agony but unable to move and effectively helpless against all his future tortures. It was also pointed out that there were no apparent defensive injuries on any of the victims – once that first spine-severing blow had been struck they were left completely at his mercy.

On 27 July he was found guilty on all counts and sentenced to spend the rest of his life in prison, with no possibility of parole.

But that was not the end of the story.

*

Almost immediately after his arrest, state-wide investigations into cold cases across New South Wales and Victoria began – focusing especially on the disappearances and unsolved murders of backpackers.

Fifty-eight historic murders were looked into, dating as far back as 1971, the same year Milat was arrested for the kidnap and rape of the 18-year-old hitchhikers. He was subsequently labelled a 'person of interest' in three of the cases, and as prime suspect in another three. Although no charges have ever been brought, he has also been linked with the disappearances and murders of a further 24 young travellers between 1972 and 1992.

Ivan Milat died in prison on 27 October 2019 without ever confessing to a single murder.

In a statement given to the press soon after the body of their daughter Joanne was found in 1992, distraught parents Ray and Gill Walters said: 'Whoever did this thing, I wouldn't call them sick, because sick people can be cured to an extent. These are evil-minded people, and like dogs with rabies there is only one way – they have got to be destroyed. There has got to be some system whereby we can destroy these people for their evil genes.'

19

DAVID & CATHERINE BIRNIE

(AUSTRALIA, 1986, 4+ VICTIMS)

David and Catherine Birnie were made for each other. They first met when they were both just 12 years old: it was to be the beginning of a lifelong love affair that would survive fractured home lives, stints in prison for both of them, and their separate marriages to other people. When they did finally reunite, 22 years after their fledgling childhood romance, it would be forever.

They were also united in blood, later dubbed Australia's answer to Fred and Rosemary West.

Together they are two of the continent's most cold-blooded, heartless serial killers, responsible for the abduction, torture, sexual assault, rape and murder of four teenagers and young women whom they snatched off the streets of Perth, Western Australia, and took home to abuse and kill at leisure – for no other reason than the satisfaction of their twisted desires. A fifth teenager escaped after being kept prisoner in their house overnight.

When asked why she had strangled one of their victims, 15-year-old high-school student Susannah Candy, Catherine Birnie claimed it had all been for love. 'I was prepared to follow him to the end of the earth and do anything to see that his desires were satisfied,' she said. 'I didn't feel a thing . . . She was a female. Females hurt and destroy males.'

*

On the afternoon of 10 November 1986, the owner of a vacuum cleaner shop in a suburb of Perth was standing outside his premises enjoying a break in business when he was startled by the sudden appearance of a barefoot, half-naked girl running headlong along the road towards him.

'Help me,' she gasped, bursting past him into the shop. 'I've been raped. Lock the door and call the police.'

At the police station she was interviewed by the only woman on duty, 22-year-old Laura Hancock, freshly graduated from the academy that winter. It was the first statement she had ever taken as a police officer. It would also be the most harrowing of her career.

The girl's name was Kate Moir and she was 17 years old. The previous evening she had been walking home from a party through the well-to-do Nedlands suburb of Perth when a car had pulled up beside her. A man and woman jumped out; he had brandished a knife and forced her into the back seat, where she was restrained and driven to a bungalow a few miles south, in the Willagee district of the city.

Once inside the house she was ordered to phone her parents to tell them she was okay, and that she was staying the night at a friend's after drinking too much. As she spoke the woman held a knife to her throat. Say anything out of character, she said, and you're dead.

Satisfied that no alarm would be raised, the couple next acted out a peculiar ritual in which Kate was made to take a shower, before being ordered to dance for them to the Dire Straits song 'Romeo and Juliet'. She was told, 'We'll only rape you if you're good.'

After the dance she was taken into the bedroom, chained to the bed, and raped twice by the man. As he assaulted her the woman watched and took notes.

By then it was past midnight – and time for bed. All three of them squeezed into the double bed together, her ankle cuffed to the man's, and she was given pills to help her sleep. She hid them under her tongue and spat them out once the couple had fallen asleep.

The following morning the man left for work, and, as Kate subsequently told Officer Hancock: 'I changed my odds to fifty-fifty, 'cos I'm just alone with the woman . . . I was very compliant, I was very nice. We listened to Dire Straits again, we watched *Rambo* together.'

Then came a knock at the door. As the woman answered, Kate was ordered back into the bedroom and to stay quiet. 'She told me to go to the room, shut up and not say a word or she'd kill me,' she said.

It was the fifty-fifty chance she'd been waiting for. Forcing a window open, Kate jumped through and ran for her life, ending up at the vacuum repair shop.

If it was an incredible story, Kate Moir also had another few surprises for Officer Hancock. During her imprisonment she had scrawled a drawing and hidden it in the house to prove she was there, and when she had taken her shower she had spotted a prescription medicine bottle in the bathroom cupboard. The name on the label: David Birnie.

Within minutes of signing her statement, Perth police were racing to the Willagee bungalow Kate claimed she had escaped from. There they found married couple David and Catherine Birnie, both 35. He was a slightly built, gaunt man, she a sharp-featured woman who looked older than her years. Neither appeared capable of kidnapping, restraining and assaulting a teenager as vibrant and intelligent as Kate Moir.

Nevertheless, in their video machine was a copy of *Rambo*, and hidden where Kate said she had left it was the scribbled drawing she had described.

The pair were taken into custody for further questioning, and once they started talking, the tale they told was worse than any of the detectives could have believed possible.

*

David Birnie and Catherine Harrison were born within a few months of each other in Western Australia in 1951, and both grew up in unusual circumstances. His parents had unconventional ideas about how to raise their children – set mealtimes were not observed, and there were rumours of prostitution, alcoholism and abuse. Meanwhile, Catherine's mother died giving birth to her younger brother when she was just two, and she was sent to live with her maternal grandparents. Eight years later, following a family dispute, she returned to her father in Perth – and the house next door to the Birnies.

The troubled children became fast friends almost immediately. Two years later the friendship grew into something more – by the age of 14 they were sleeping together and, perhaps seeing themselves as renegade lovers in the style of Bonnie and Clyde, their romance was also defined by increasing acts of lawlessness that began with shoplifting and escalated into a string of burglaries. Inevitably, they both ended up in youth detention centres; David's crimes included the attempted rape of an elderly lady.

Prison separated them, and despite continuing to write hundreds of letters to each other, both met and married other partners in their early twenties – in Catherine's case to the son of the man who employed her as a housekeeper, with whom she had seven children.

Like the star-crossed lovers on whom they had modelled themselves as young teenagers, however, they simply couldn't live apart. Their correspondence had continued even through their separate marriages, and in 1985 both abruptly left their spouses and moved in together, to a bungalow on Moorhouse Street, Willagee. Although they never legally married, she changed her name by deed poll to Birnie, and they told everyone they were husband and wife.

If an adolescent ideal of living as romantic outlaws had defined their young relationship, by the time of their reunion they were in their mid-thirties and had to at least maintain a respectable façade. David worked at a car wrecker's yard near their Willagee home, Catherine played the doting housewife.

Behind closed doors it was a different story.

Despite his diminutive appearance, David was a voracious sexual animal, addicted to violent pornography and near insatiable in his appetite for increasingly outlandish ways of getting his kicks, often demanding sex up to six times a day. Catherine, devoted to fulfilling her lover's every desire, did her best, but simply couldn't keep up.

Within a year of reuniting they decided to do something about it.

*

Their first idea for finding a suitable subject on whom David could live out the most extreme of his sexual perversions was almost laughably unsubtle – it was to literally advertise for someone by taking out a notice in the local newspaper. Although apparently innocuous, with the benefit of hindsight, the wording of their advertisement holds a chilling hidden meaning.

'URGENT', it read. 'Looking for a lonely young person. Prefer female 18 to 24 years, share single flat.' The advertisement yielded no responses – perhaps because of that sinister insistence on 'lonely'.

When the couple did finally strike, their method was even less subtle. David had met 22-year-old university student Mary Neilsen at the wrecker's yard, where he told her he could source cut-price tyres for her car. On 6 October 1986 she stopped by the Birnies' house to collect them.

David answered the door with a knife in his hand, hauling her inside before she could scream for help, and forcing her through to the bedroom. Her hands and feet were chained to the bed, a gag bound over her mouth, and, as Catherine watched, he raped her.

When he was done, she was bundled into the boot of their car and driven 40 minutes out of town, to the edge of Gleneagle State Forest. There David raped her again, strangling her with a nylon cord as he climaxed. She was buried in a shallow grave, and before covering her up, David insisted they repeatedly stab her dead body in the belief that blood loss and open wounds would speed up decomposition.

The next morning he went to work as usual and for the following days the couple kept a low profile, carefully monitoring the news to see if any connection had been made between the missing student and the car wrecker's yard.

After two weeks they decided they had got away with it, and

went in search of another young target. When it came it was almost too easy.

David and Catherine had been cruising the streets of Perth for hours on the evening of 20 October when they saw 15-year-old Susannah Candy hitching a lift home in the Claremont district, just a short drive from their home. They pulled over, offered her a lift, and, reassured by the presence of a woman in the car, Susannah jumped in.

As soon as she was in the car a knife was held to her throat and her hands tied. Minutes later they had pulled up in Moorhouse Street and, in a repeat of the abuses inflicted upon Mary Neilsen, she was gagged, chained to the bed and repeatedly raped. Unlike with Neilsen, however, the assaults were not only inflicted by David; this time Catherine joined in.

The Birnies were reluctant to finish with their new plaything quite so quickly as they had with their first victim. Over the following two days she was kept prisoner, only released from her chains to visit the toilet – always accompanied by either David or Catherine – or else to write letters dictated by the couple to her family to reassure them that she was staying with friends.

Finally, David grew tired of her – and instructed Catherine to show her love for him by putting the girl out of her misery. She was only too happy to prove herself, pulling and twisting the nylon cord tighter and tighter, watching fascinated as the child's eyes bulged and her cheeks turned purple, until finally the job was done. She too was taken to Gleneagle, and buried alongside Neilsen.

In David and Catherine Birnie's minds, the abduction, imprisonment, abuse and murder of two victims in as many weeks had proved they could get away with anything. Finding girls was easy; chaining them up and raping them was easy; killing and burying them was easy. And doing it all without anyone suspecting a thing . . . easy.

They found their next victim standing by the side of the road just 10 days after disposing of Susannah Candy.

Thirty-one-year-old Noelene Patterson had pulled over after running out of petrol on her way home from work on 1 November. After ostensibly stopping to help her, David and Catherine bundled her into their vehicle, subduing her at knifepoint, before taking her back to the bungalow to become their latest prisoner.

Noelene suffered for three days as the Birnies' sex slave, kept chained in their bedroom while David repeatedly raped her, returning again and again to violate her in increasingly violent assaults. So frequent and prolonged were his attacks that Catherine even grew jealous of the attention he was showing Noelene.

She gave him an ultimatum – and this time it was David's turn to prove his love.

He didn't hesitate. After forcing a fistful of sleeping pills down her throat, he strangled Noelene as she passed out, and she joined the bodies at their Gleneagle graveyard. Catherine insisted on being the one to throw the first shovelfuls of dirt on the body.

Two days after burying Noelene Patterson, and by now

feeling untouchable, the pair snatched 21-year-old Denise Brown from a bus stop. She was kept overnight, before being taken, still alive, to a new burial ground, a pine plantation to the north of the city.

As they waited on the edge of the forest for night to fall, David passed the time by raping her in the front seat of the car, and then, once satisfied that it was dark enough outside, raped her again in the forest, before stabbing her in the neck and digging a grave.

Denise was not dead yet. As they threw her into the ground, she groaned, raised an arm, tried to sit up. Cool as ice, Catherine handed her lover an axe: he swung it twice at the girl's head. The first blow killed her, the second made sure of it.

As they drove home, the mood was exultant. For our next target, David Birnie told his devoted wife, I want someone younger again. Another teenager.

Three days later they found Kate Moir, walking home from her party in Nedlands.

*

Once the Birnies had been arrested, they confessed almost immediately, with David even claiming that he regretted the suffering he had caused. In court, charged with four counts of murder and one count each of abduction and rape, he went so far as to declare that he entered a guilty plea out of compassion, to spare the families of his victims a long trial, telling them, 'It's the least I could do.'

If nobody was buying the contrition as genuine, the casualness with which both David and Catherine Birnie accepted their arrests was, if anything, more frightening than if they had denied, or tried to justify their actions. They simply didn't seem to care. Both were sentenced to spend the rest of their lives in prison.

On 7 October 2005, David Birnie was found hanging in his prison cell. Prior to his suicide he had been described as a 'model prisoner'.

Catherine Birnie remains behinds bars. In 2017 her youngest son from her first marriage publicly called for her execution. When asked what his last words to his mother would be, he replied: 'Hurry up and die.'

20

HAROLD SHIPMAN

(UK, 1975–98, 218–50 VICTIMS)

octor Harold Shipman was Britain's worst serial killer –
and one of the most prolific murderers to have ever lived.
The sheer number of people he killed is astonishing –
initially convicted of the murders of 15 individuals, an inquiry
set up after his eventual arrest and incarceration uncovered a
campaign of death that spanned 23 years and accounted for at
least 218 victims. All were patients under his care as a doctor,
most of them middle-aged and elderly ladies; all trusted him
implicitly. He used his position as a well-loved and respected
general practitioner to win their confidence, and then he used
that same status to administer them fatal doses of powerful
opioid painkillers, forge their death certificates and alter their

medical notes to record they passed away of natural causes.

With one notable exception, he did not kill for money, or from anger, or hate, or revenge, or mental illness, or any of the other usual reasons mass murderers target their victims. To this day, 20 years after he hanged himself in his prison cell, speculation as to his 'why?' continues.

Harold Shipman's body count exceeds that of any British serial killer by nearly 200 people – his closest rival, the nineteenth-century poisoner Jonathan Balls, accounted for 22 deaths before his own suicide – but when you take into account who his victims were, how he was able to murder them, and the calm, methodical manner in which he went about it, the scale and severity of his crimes exceeds even the breathtaking numbers involved.

He was not like other serial killers. His victims did not die in terror, begging for mercy. They died believing he was helping them.

*

Harold Shipman should have been struck off the medical register in 1975, when he was caught forging prescriptions of the painkiller pethidine for his own use. He had been working in his first position as a general practitioner at a doctors' surgery in Todmorden, West Yorkshire, for a year, but had also developed a serious addiction to opioids since his time at Leeds Medical School 10 years earlier.

As a doctor he could effectively sign off prescriptions with next to no checks or scrutiny – and he had abused that privilege to feed his habit for six months before a local pharmacist raised concerns about the sheer volume of pethidine prescriptions that were being authorized by the same young GP.

Shipman was fined just £600 on drugs and forgery charges, but received no censure from the General Medical Council. Instead, he spent time at a drug rehabilitation centre near York, and two years later, somehow concealing his criminal record, joined a practice at a medical centre in Hyde, Greater Manchester.

By then he had already started killing. For this too, opioids were his drug of choice.

Harold Shipman's first experience with opioids – the medical name for a class of drugs naturally found in the opium poppy plant and that, as well as including prescribed drugs like codeine and morphine, also encompasses synthetic derivatives such as heroin – came when he was just a teenager.

Growing up, he enjoyed an especially close relationship with his mother, and when she fell ill with lung cancer, he was devastated. As her health worsened, she was brought home for end-of-life care: he watched as the family doctor would visit daily to administer her morphine, and he couldn't help but note the relief the drug brought her.

She died when he was 17 years old, and if the seeds of his own addiction were planted in her final weeks, so too may have been the basis of his later murders.

Three years after his mother's death, he married Primrose Oxtoby in 1966 while still a student at Leeds, and after graduating he worked at a hospital in Pontefract, Yorkshire, before joining the Todmorden practice as assistant principal GP. He and Primrose remained married for the rest of his life, and had four children together.

On 10 May 1974, two months after starting in Todmorden, Shipman signed his first ever death certificate. Seventy-two-year-old Ruth Highley had passed away, according to that certificate, of kidney failure. Fifty years on, it is impossible to know how true that may have been – and following the 2002 publication of *The Shipman Inquiry*, questions have been raised about the deaths of eight more of his Todmorden patients before his dismissal in 1975. In each case he not only signed the death certificates, but is thought to have been present when they died.

*

When Dr Shipman arrived at the Donnybrook House practice in October 1977 aged 31, the people of Hyde took to their new GP immediately. In the close-knit working-class community, he was a breath of fresh air, young and handsome, ready to volunteer at local events and fundraisers, and possessed of a seemingly endless capacity for caring, thoughtful and expert diagnoses of their ailments. Such was his considerate and patient bedside manner that, for his elderly patients, home visits – which he was always more than happy to conduct – became something they looked forward to.

Unbeknown to everyone, he was also steadily and methodically murdering those same patients who put such trust in him. According to the later inquiry, he is thought to have first struck within just weeks of starting at Donnybrook House; over the next 15 years at the practice, he killed another 80 of his patients there.

His method was deceptively simple, and devastatingly effective. He injected each of his victims with a lethal dose of the opioid diamorphine, a powerful painkiller most commonly used to help terminal cancer patients. In small doses it can help sufferers breathe easier – take too much and it is fatal, its effects akin to a heroin overdose.

The diamorphine he used had been carefully stockpiled especially for carrying out his killings, Shipman once again using his position as a GP to fill out countless false prescriptions or else simply stealing supplies of the drug from deceased cancer patients.

Once his victim had slipped into unconsciousness, death would quickly follow. As their doctor it would be his responsibility to fill in their death certificates; inevitably, the official record would state they died of natural causes, pre-existing medical conditions, or viral infections such as pneumonia.

In 1993, Shipman left Donnybrook House to set up his own practice almost within sight of his old surgery. Such was his standing in the community that the majority of his patients followed him; and the same year he was even featured in the long-running current affairs documentary series *World in Action* as an expert on how mentally ill patients should be cared for and integrated into society.

Once established in his new solo practice, Shipman could effectively operate with no checks or balances on his behaviour. By the time he was finally arrested he had nearly 3,000 patients on his books – and the death rate among his elderly patients was three times higher than the norm for the Hyde area.

For six more years he continued his deadly double life – to the public the well-respected family man and caring GP, always ready to check in on his most vulnerable patients on the way to his surgery in the mornings or else on his regular rounds in the afternoons; and in secret, a precise and dispassionate serial killer who would reassure his victims that he could help with their pain even as he loaded the syringes that would kill them.

With this apparent impunity came an arrogance. The daughter of one patient would recall how when she came to collect her mother's death certificate he had all but taunted her.

'I told him my mum's name and explained that I wanted her death certificate,' she said, as reported by the *Manchester Evening News*. 'He started scribbling on a piece of paper and he said, "I think we will put it down to pneumonia." As he wrote this, he started to laugh.'

Finally, in March 1998, the sheer number of deaths in the Hyde area started to attract attention. Local undertakers and paramedics began to talk of his surgery as having a reputation for losing an unusually high number of its patients, and after Dr Lisa Reynolds of a neighbouring medical practice raised concerns with the chief coroner for South Manchester about the number of cremation forms for elderly women that

Shipman had been asking her to countersign, an investigation was launched.

A month later, the investigation was closed again due to a lack of evidence; and Harold Shipman continued as before. He would kill three more times before his grisly hold over the people of Hyde was brought to a dramatic end.

*

By the time Shipman murdered his final victim, wealthy former mayor of Hyde Kathleen Grundy, it is estimated he was killing his patients at a rate of around one a week.

Kathleen Grundy was 81 years old but known to be an energetic, lively woman who maintained a healthy social life despite her age. On the morning of 24 June 1998, Shipman had called in at her house on the way to the surgery to take a blood sample for what he said was an ageing survey being conducted by Manchester University. Just hours later she was found dead on her sofa. As her doctor, Shipman duly recorded her official cause of death as old age.

The same day, a local firm of solicitors received a copy of her will. 'All my estate, money and home to my doctor,' it read. 'My family are not in need and I want to reward him for all the care he has given to me and the people of Hyde.'

The estimated value of those assets was £386,000.

When Kathleen's daughter Angela Woodruff, herself a solicitor, saw the will, she was immediately suspicious. Why would her mother leave nearly £400,000 to her doctor? And, come to think of it, how is it that such a sprightly and active woman could suddenly come to die of old age? She took her suspicions to the police, and for the second time that year, an investigation into Dr Shipman was launched.

This time, the police were more thorough. Mrs Grundy's body was exhumed and underwent a comprehensive post-mortem, which revealed traces of diamorphine in her bloodstream. When police presented that evidence to Shipman he claimed the 81-year-old was a heroin addict, even showing them notes to that effect that he had made on her computerized medical record.

When detectives examined the computer, they found he had written the entries after her death, and on 7 September 1998 he was arrested on suspicion of killing Kathleen Grundy and forging her will. Police later described the attempted forgery as 'cack-handed': the fake will had been typed on a typewriter kept in his surgery, and his fingerprints were all over the document.

With the previous concerns raised about the unusually high mortality rate among Shipman's patients still fresh in detectives' minds, the police also investigated an initial 15 further deaths of middle-aged and elderly women under his care, and found that in each case he had administered fatal doses of diamorphine, before attributing their deaths to natural causes on official certificates and posthumously amending their medical records to suggest long-standing health conditions.

On 31 January 2000, he was found guilty of all 15 counts of murder and sentenced to spend the rest of his life in prison. Eleven days later, finally, the General Medical Council struck him off the medical register.

*

Over the following years the true scale of the horror would finally be revealed.

Immediately after his jailing, the Shipman Inquiry was launched to investigate every one of the 459 people who had died while under his care in Yorkshire and Manchester: in 2002 it concluded that he had killed no fewer than 218 times between 1975 and 1998. Nearly half of all of his patients that had passed away in those 23 years had been murdered by Harold Shipman.

A further report in 2005 suggested that the final tally could be as high as 250 and that he may even have begun killing while still a medical student in 1971.

By the time that final report was issued, Shipman was already dead. On 13 January 2004 he hanged himself with his bed sheets in his cell. Few mourned.

His death did, however, leave a wealth of unanswered questions . . . the first of which was what drove him, after at least 217 successful murders, to attempt such a clumsy and amateurish forging of a will? Was his arrogance by that time so out of control that he genuinely believed he would get away with it? Or was he unconsciously trying to get caught as a kind of cry for help, so lost in his own depravity that he wanted to do something, anything, to make it stop? Only one man could have ever told us that; and now he never will.

Harold Shipman will be forever remembered as one of the worst men to have lived. During his three decades as a GP and a murderer, he stands apart from almost every other serial killer in history – for the sheer number of people he murdered, for the 23 years he was able to kill without censure, and for the fact that the very people he marked out for death trusted and respected him.

But at the same time he also remains defined by the one question that unites every serial killer.

Whatever the means and methods they used, whatever the psychological or social troubles they lived with, whatever rages or perversions drove their need to murder, all serial killers ultimately leave us with a 'why?'.

For Doctor Harold Shipman, as with so many other serial killers, it is a question that will never be truly answered. Perhaps there is no answer. Perhaps, in some, evil simply exists.

ACKNOWLEDGEMENTS

The author is indebted to a wealth of resources in the writing of this book, especially the Associated Press and the BBC, as well as online resources including: crimelibrary.org, biography.com, murderpedia.com, serialkillercalendar.com, victimsofhomicide. fandom.com and Britannica.com. Additionally, the books, articles, TV broadcasts, court records and police files, as listed in the bibliography that follows, have proved invaluable.

BIBLIOGRAPHY

BOOKS

Appleyard, Nick, *Life Means Life: Jailed Forever – True Stories of Britain's Most Evil Killers* (John Blake, 2009)

Dwyer, Kevin, *True Stories of Law & Order: Special Victims Unit – The Real Crimes Behind the Best Episodes of the Hit TV Show* (Berkley, 2007)

Fawkes, Sandy, *Natural Born Killer* (Blake Publishing, 2004)

Gilmour, Walter and Hale, Leland E., *Butcher, Baker: The True Account of an Alaskan Serial Killer* (Open Road Media, 2018)

Kerr, Gordon, *World Serial Killers* (Canary Press, 2011)

Kidd, Paul, *Australia's Serial Killers: The Definitive History of Serial Multicide in Australia* (Pan Macmillan, 2006)

Lauren, Jillian, *Behold the Monster: Facing America's Most Prolific Serial Killer* (Ebury Press, 2022)

Lee, Carol Ann, *One of Your Own: The Life and Death of Myra Hindley* (Mainstream Publishing, 2010)

Masters, Brian, *Killing for Company* (Cornerstone, 2011)

Newton, Michael, *Hunting Humans: Encyclopedia of Modern Serial Killers* (Avon Books, 1992)

Ritchie, Jean, *Myra Hindley: Inside the Mind of a Murderess* (Angus & Robertson, 1988)

Whittaker, Mark, *Sins of the Brother: The Definitive Story of Ivan Milat and the Backpacker Murders* (Macmillan, 1998)

NEWS ARTICLES

'The road to Imperial Avenue', *The Plain Dealer*, 24 January 2010

'Serial killer Anthony Sowell began raping niece when both were children, witness testifies', Cleveland.com, 2 August 2011

'John Wayne Gacy, 40 years later', *Chicago Tribune*, 16 December 2018

'Conversations with a killer', *New Yorker*, 10 April 1994

'John Wayne Gacy speaks', CBS Chicago, 20 January 2012

'The Dennis Nilsen case', *Guardian*, 5 November 1983

'Cold killer: Where is Rose West now?' *Sun*, 21 August 2023

'Gruesome trail of killing', *The Age* (Australia), 9 September 2003

'Gloating over a victim's grave', *Daily Mail*, 18 May 2017

'Indiana serial killer's victims still unknown long after his death', revealnews.org, 29 September 2015

'Apology at sentencing deepens mystery of Golden State Killer', AP News, 22 August 2020

'Fingering a killer', *Orange Coast* magazine, October 1988

'How the "Golden State Killer", a serial rapist, murderer, evaded capture for decades', ABC News, 31 October 2020

'Why "Golden State Killer" may have stopped murder spree', ABC News, 3 May 2018

'The Golden State Killer: How it took four decades to catch the serial predator who terrorised California', abc.net.au, 21 August 2020

'Survivors band together to have their cold cases reviewed again after Golden State Killer sentencing', Fox40 News, 31 August 2020

'The serial killer and the "less dead": The only reporter who's talked to Samuel Little tells how he was caught – and why he almost got away', *New York Magazine*, 20 December 2018

'Who is the most prolific serial killer in history? Everything we know about Samuel Little', Oxygen True Crime, 24 May 2023

'Wuornos' last words: "I'll be back"', CNN, 15 October 2002

'The true story of serial killer Aileen Wuornos', Grunge.com, 1 February 2023

'The banality of Gary: A Green River chiller', *Washington Post*, 16 November 2003

'Arrest in Green River murders', *Los Angeles Times*, 1 December 2001

'How a crime lab missed evidence that could have stopped the Green River Killer', NBC News, 3 March 2023

'Timeline of many of Ted Bundy's brutal crimes', ABC News, 15 February 2019

'My anger is buried deep inside', *Guardian*, 21 February 2008

'Ipswich prostitute murders: The victims', *Telegraph*, 21 February 2008

'A secret life in the red light district . . . then came the urge to kill', *Guardian*, 22 February 2008

'Robert Hansen: The Alaskan serial killer who hunted his victims like animals', Allthatsinteresting.com, 24 November 2021

'Robert Hansen dies at 75: convicted Alaska serial killer', WashingtonPost.com, 22 August 2014

'Hunting humans', David Lohr, Crimelibrary.com

'Who is Reta Mays? Nursing assistant kills 7 vets with lethal jabs, watch them die', *International Business Times*, 25 July 2020

'Interviewing a killer: Federal investigators shed light on Reta Mays case', *Metro News*, West Virginia, 17 October 2021

'Angel of death: Reta Mays', Medium.com, 20 February 2022

'The timeline of Reta Mays' crimes and what's next', WDTV, West Virginia, 15 July 2020

'Knowles' slayings in state described', *Hartford Courant*, 30 January 1975

'Date with the devil: "Casanova killer" Paul John Knowles spared Fleet Street reporter Sandy Fawkes', *New York Daily News*, 24 April 2010

'Milledgeville shocked, Mandy, father, killed by "maniacs"?', *The Atlanta Constitution*, 8 November 1974

'From netball team to psychopath: The strange descent of Joanna Dennehy', *Guardian*, 12 February 2014

'Joanne Dennehy: What makes a female serial killer tick', *The Week*, 10 February 2014

'The Story of Joanna Dennehy, the sadistic serial killer who butchered three men "for fun"', Allthatsinteresting.com, 30 July 2022

'Trophies of a serial killer', *Daily Mail*, 21 May 2014

'"How I escaped the house of horrors": Hostage of Australia's most evil killers tells how she fled', Yahoo News, 29 March 2018

'Serial killer dubbed "Australian Rose West": Rape, murder and parole attempts', *Daily Mirror*, 2 September 2021

'"You know you're gonna die": How a teen survived Australia's worst serial killer couple', Mamamia, 5 February 2017

'Portrait of a necrophiliac', *Guardian*, 13 January 2004

'Why did Harold Shipman kill more than 250 of his patients?', *Telegraph*, 26 April 2018

'Josephine not Shipman's first Manchester victim', *Manchester Evening News*, 30 April 2005

OTHER SOURCES

The Nilsen Files, BBC News (BBC Two), 20 January 2022

'Unmasking the Golden State Killer: Dark investigation into Joseph DeAngelo', *60 Minutes* (Australia), 29 June 2020

Alaska: Ice Cold Killers, Investigation Discovery, 25 January 2012

R v. BUNTING & OTHERS (NO. 3), Supreme Court of South Australia, 29 October 2003

The People of the State of Illinois v. Larry Eyler, Supreme Court of Illinois, 25 October 1989

Ted Bundy Multiagency Investigative Team Report, US Department of Justice Federal Bureau of Investigation, 1992